WRESTLING WITH GOD

RIVER
OAK
PUBLISHING

Wrestling with God:
10 Stories of Modern Day Warriors Who Came Face to Face with the Creator
ISBN 1-58919-935-9
Copyright © 2001 by Chad Bonham

Published by RiverOak Publishing
P.O. Box 700143
Tulsa, Oklahoma 74170-0143

CHAD BONHAM

RIVER
OAK
PUBLISHING
Tulsa, Oklahoma

ACKNOWLEDGMENTS

I would like to thank the many people who have inspired and encouraged me to reach for my highest goals—specifically my parents, Stan and Betty Bonham, and my sisters, Rhonda Dilldine and Karla Partridge, and their families.

I would especially like to express my gratitude to Mark Gilroy, Jeff Dunn, Christina Honea, Debbie Justus, Monica Hamilton, and the entire RiverOak staff for being willing to take a chance on what most thought was a risky concept and for giving a rookie author a chance to fulfill a dream. It's been a pleasure working with each and every one of you.

My thanks also go to numerous friends for their support in all of my past and present endeavors. Special thanks to my Clear Channel and Live 101.5 KMRX family for supporting my efforts away from the radio station.

Finally, I want to thank the two most important people in my life: my incredible wife, Amy, for her undying support and God-inspired patience, and my Lord and Savior Jesus Christ. This is truly for You. I can't imagine what You have planned for me next, but I'm looking forward to it with great anticipation.

TABLE OF CONTENTS

INTRODUCTION

Jake wasn't expecting to make history that night. He was simply killing time staring up at the clear, star-filled sky—dreading the arrival of tomorrow. His double-crossing ways were about to catch up to him, and he feared what punishment awaited. Suddenly, from out of the darkness, an unannounced guest appeared.

With only the faint light supplied by the moon, Jake had trouble distinguishing the approaching man's face. His fading eyesight certainly didn't help matters. But Jake's survival instincts were still sharp, and he sensed quickly that his visitor meant business. He had a long night ahead of him.

Before Jake could react, the daunting figure invaded his space. Sizing each other up, the two adversaries locked arms and prepared for battle. The mystery man quickly took the upper hand, putting Jake into a constricting headlock. With every ounce of strength he could muster, Jake managed to flip his opponent onto his back. Jake lunged, and the two rolled around on the grainy desert sand for several minutes. Back and forth, back and forth—the fight turned first one way, then the other as each man would temporarily take control of the match. Jake was clearly at a disadvantage in strength, but his determination was enough to keep him alive—for the time being.

There was no raucous crowd cheering either competitor on to victory, just a host of curious creatures enjoying the show. Jake and his foe were engaged in a street brawl of sorts with no referee present to ensure a clean fight. Jake took advantage of that fact by trying to choke his attacker. It didn't last long. The stronger and apparently much younger man flung Jake away, sending his body airborne. Jake hit the ground with a thud. With the wind knocked out of him, his unrelenting opponent mercilessly began to put him through a series of submission holds. But Jake refused to give up. He knew he couldn't fast-talk his way out of this predicament. There was no deal available for the making. This was literally a do-or-die situation.

The two opponents continued to struggle long into the night. As the dark sky began to fade to gray and the rising sun began to glimmer on the horizon, Jake—weakened and breathless—could only clutch and grab at his adversary with occasional bursts of energy. Though his strength was waning, Jake determined to make a fight of it until the end. His opponent, though obviously superior in strength and skill, could not dispatch Jake.

Then, inexplicably, the unnamed warrior suddenly released his hold on Jake and rose from the ground. He had given up. Or had he? Disoriented and confused, Jake attempted to stand.

Watching his mysterious opponent disappear into the fading darkness, Jake realized he had actually survived. He had won the greatest fight of his life . . . but not without paying a price. His hip was dislocated and his stride noticeably hindered, causing him to grimace in pain with every step he attempted. Jake would suffer from this injury for the rest of his life, yet he limped away from the scene of the contest with a sense of pride in a victory earned. This was an odd feeling for a man who had spent most of his life trying to avoid any hard work or honest achievement.

You may be wondering who this unremarkable, anti-hero might be. This is the true story of Jacob of Old Testament fame. It's the same Jacob who swindled his older brother, Esau, out of his birthright, the same Jacob who ran like a coward from his family in fear of his life. It's the same Jacob who outsmarted himself and inherited the burdensome task of dealing with two competing wives, Rachel and Leah. And this very night, as he nervously awaited the next day's meeting with his estranged sibling, Jacob made history by becoming the world's very first recorded wrestler.

Some believe Jacob was wrestling an angel that night. Others suggest he was wrestling God Himself. His mysterious opponent named him "Israel," which means "he who wrestles God." This may be a not-so-subtle hint that the latter interpretation is most likely the more correct of the two. Regardless of who his opponent was, Jacob's story is certainly worthy of the modern-day wrestling ring. Along with a host of related themes, such as deceit, jealousy, greed, and betrayal, his life attributes read like a list of titles for upcoming wrestling pay-per-view events.

Now the twenty-first century is in full swing, and professional wrestling is a thriving industry that crosses almost every cultural line. Professional wrestlers are an unusual hybrid: part action hero, part athlete, and part superhero ... with a little make-believe thrown in. Past superstars such as Hulk Hogan, Andre the Giant, Bret "The Hitman" Hart, Rowdy Roddy Piper, and the Ultimate Warrior spurred a huge wrestling revival and paved the way for today's hugely popular anti-heroes.

Whether you picked up *Wrestling with God* as an avid wrestling fan or simply out of curiosity, my hope is that you will be both entertained and inspired. These are true, personal stories about men who have competed at the highest level of professional wrestling, under the bright lights and in front of raving, manic crowds. Each one achieved his dream—to contend in the ring— only to discover there was still something missing in his life.

They are stories of triumph and defeat, pleasure and pain, transgression and forgiveness. This is about *real* life—not created storylines, make-believe characters, or gimmicks. They are stories of men who, like Jacob, could justifiably be re-named "Israel," because each one has wrestled with God and walked away with a greater reward than any title belt could ever fulfill.

It is my desire that as you read this book, you will see the parallel between these men's lives and your own search for truth, happiness, and hope. I hope the transformations that you are about to witness will inspire you and maybe even leave you changed. In one way or another, we all are wrestling with God.

TATANKA

CHAPTER 1

I t began just like every other Sunday morning church service at Touch of God Ministries in St. Petersburg, Florida. The people worshipped joyfully and lifted up their prayers to God. Little did Chris Chavis know that on this particular morning God would command his attention in a powerful and awesome way. Better known as Tatanka, the former World Wrestling Federation superstar had experienced many personal encounters with God. Tatanka knew God could change a life for the better, but today he would witness God's power in a new, miraculous way.

As the people sang a familiar chorus in unison, an older man suddenly collapsed in the aisle. Two church members, a paramedic and a nurse, rushed to assist him, rolling him onto his back and checking his vital signs. "He doesn't have a pulse!" the paramedic cried. "Oh my God, he doesn't have a pulse!"

Tatanka and another church leader quickly ran over to help. The man's breathing had long since stopped; his lips and face slowly started to turn blue. As the man's wife began to weep, Pastor Harry Lyum calmly took charge. "Church, stay calm and start praying," he said.

Tatanka began to wonder just how this story was going to play out. In the ring, he had wrestled a "dead man" before, namely The Undertaker, who portrayed a zombie-like character early in his career. But this wasn't a work of fiction or part of a wrestling story-line. This was God's turf, and the man he was standing over this time was really dead.

After what seemed like just minutes shy of eternity, Pastor Lyum casually walked over to the man lying motionless on the floor. Sensing a nudge from the Holy Spirit, the pastor knelt down and placed his hands on the man's chest. "I said 'live' in the name of Jesus!" he commanded. Instantly, the man's stomach lifted up as a rush of air filled his lungs. Needless to say, Touch of God Ministries didn't dismiss at noon for lunch on this miraculous Sunday, and Tatanka found his life changed once again by the strength and unmatched power of God.

Since rededicating his life to Christ in 1996, Tatanka has wit-nessed and experienced countless miracles. He has seen angels and encountered demonic spirits. But after spending four years away from mainstream professional wrestling, he began to wonder if God was planning on resurrecting his wrestling career, too. Would God really use him in an industry that was choking on its own excess? Could he help usher in a new and more wholesome era? Certainly, Tatanka had a fresh outlook on life and a powerful new message to share with the millions of wrestling fans worldwide.

"People need to know that the truth is Jesus," Tatanka says. "He is the way to life. He will bless you abundantly. He wants to see you happy. He doesn't want to see what He created on the earth being miserable."

Tatanka used to think he could do anything if he only believed in himself. Born June 8, 1960, in Pembroke, North Carolina, to Stoney and Patricia Chavis, Tatanka embraced his heritage as a full-blooded Lumbee Indian from an early age. The Lumbee Tribe is the largest tribe east of the Mississippi River

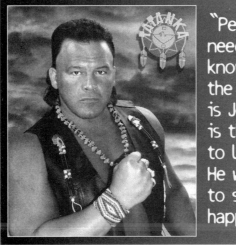

"People need to know that the truth is Jesus. He is the way to life . . . He wants to see you happy."

and ninth largest in the United States, and while noted for a wealth of successful businessmen, lawyers, doctors, and politicians, the tribe proudly hails Tatanka as one of its most famous athletes.

During his childhood, Tatanka and his family routinely attended church, but it wasn't until his sixteenth birthday that Tatanka first encountered God in a personal way. The family had moved to Hampton, Virginia, and that memorable Sunday they attended a morning service at Liberty Baptist Church.

"This presence of God came over me so strong," Tatanka recalls. "It was so powerful on me. It was like electricity or lightning all over me. Without even thinking about it, something just had me jump up. As I was walking to the altar, I could hardly stand. I was shaking, and I was sobbing."

Although Tatanka accepted Christ that day, he gradually fell back into his old way of life. He had never been a bad kid, but without any spiritual discipleship or training, his interest in God waned. Other teenage pursuits captured his interest, and he excelled in everything he attempted. Tatanka was a star football player and a member of the 1976 Virginia State Championship team. He earned A's and B's in school and climbed the ROTC ladder all the way to brigade commander. By the time his senior year came to a close, athletic offers were pouring in from the University of North Carolina, the University of Tennessee, the University of Virginia, and James Madison University, among others.

Tatanka chose to attend James Madison, but even before enrolling, he knew it would be a short stay. Tatanka planned to earn a two-year degree and then move on to something new. However, he only lasted a year before his restless spirit brought him back to Hampton. At the age of nineteen, he took on a job working with his father on nuclear aircraft carriers and submarines at a Newport News shipyard.

Several jobs followed, and soon Tatanka was working sixteen hours a day and making it on his own. Then Tatanka's life took an unexpected turn. After spending three months working on a fishing boat, Tatanka followed some friends to Fort Lauderdale, Florida, where bodybuilding was a popular sport. Always interested in keeping in shape, he had placed a greater emphasis on powerlifting while living in Virginia. That all changed when he first stepped into a gym and realized the muscle definition a human body was capable of achieving.

As he trained for amateur competitions, Tatanka developed a growing interest in the health and fitness industry. Eventually, Tatanka took a job selling memberships at Bally's Health Club. He quickly pushed himself to the top of the company with a sales average of $100,000 per month and was one of two finalists for a major promotion. Tatanka's income was so lucrative that he turned down an opportunity to play for the Miami Dolphins after making the cut at a free agent tryout.

In the meantime, Tatanka had become acquainted with wrestler and promoter Bobby "The Kid" Rogers. One day the two struck up a conversation at a neighborhood Blockbuster Video store. Rogers was impressed with Tatanka's look and encouraged him to consider professional wrestling as a career. Tatanka knew little about the sport, but curiosity caused him to return and rent wrestling videos to research. He and Rogers would occasionally bump into one another at the video rack. During one such meeting, Rogers invited Tatanka to meet the original "Nature Boy," Buddy Rogers.

"Every time I'd see Bobby, he started baiting that hook," Tatanka says. "I'm not someone who can be hooked easily, but I did start watching wrestling on Saturday mornings. WWF was unbelievably hot. The more I watched these guys, it started to hit me. The arenas were sold out. The crowd response was huge. These guys were celebrities, and the merchandise was selling. I started to look at it as a business move."

It took Tatanka a while to warm up to the idea, but he finally agreed to meet with the elder Rogers. The wrestling pioneer had connections in the business and immediately pegged the Native American as a future star. Rogers tossed names around like WWF president Vince McMahon and former WWF booker George Scott. Still, Tatanka remained uncertain about making such a drastic move. He didn't need the money and had already bought a house and new car. There had to be a greater enticement for Tatanka to dive into the ring.

"Buddy Rogers actually walked right into my office and made the pitch," Tatanka remembers. "He told me I needed to do it. He planted that seed in me. Now it was in me, and I knew that if I didn't do it right then, it was going to be in the back of my mind for the rest of my life."

Tatanka's decision was met with great resistance on multiple fronts. His parents were especially displeased.

"Stoney! He's lost his mind," Tatanka heard his mother Patricia yell over the phone. "You need to talk some sense into your boy! He's lost his mind!"

"You're a fool!" his father chastised Tatanka after grabbing the phone from his wife. "That's a dream. It will never happen."

Actually, a less emotional response would have shocked Tatanka more. He expected and even understood their disapproval.

Many experts still consider Tatanka to be the fastest-rising star ever in WWF history

"My parents were looking out for me because I was making $100,000 a year," Tatanka says. "I understood where they were coming from. But they'd never taken the time to step back and look at everything I'd accomplished up to that point. I'm not saying anything bad against my parents, but no matter what anybody says, I knew as long I believed in myself, I could accomplish anything."

Rogers sent Tatanka northeast to Larry Sharpe's Monster Factory in New Jersey, a well-respected wrestling training center that also produced such notables as Bam Bam Bigelow, King Kong Bundy,

Mike Jones (a.k.a. Virgil or Vincent) and WWF superstar Charles Wright (a.k.a. Papa Shango, The Godfather, or The Goodfather). On weekends, while the others were out partying, Tatanka would borrow Sharpe's key to the school and put in extra time with one of the teachers. He spent three quick months there before graduating to the next level. During his stay, he saw his first official action by defeating Joe Thunderstorm in a World Wrestling Alliance (WWA) match in Philadelphia.

Turning down a management contract from Sharpe, Tatanka returned home from his crash course. He met up with Rogers, who immediately took him to see George Scott. The former WWF employee was starting a new promotion called the North American Wrestling Association. It would later become known as South Atlantic Pro Wrestling (SAPW) and would boast such talent as Ricky "The Dragon" Steamboat, John Studd, the Nasty Boys, and Ken Shamrock. Tatanka packed his bags and moved to Charlotte, North Carolina, where the promotion was based.

In one year with Scott, Tatanka showed the stuff that champions are made of while performing as "War Eagle" Chris Chavis. He became the SAPW Heavyweight Champion by defeating Shamrock in Lumberton, North Carolina. Tatanka was also voted runner-up for 1990 Rookie of the Year by *Pro Wrestling Illustrated*. It wasn't long before McMahon and the WWF took notice. In fact, many experts still consider Tatanka to be the fastest-rising star ever in WWF history.

The timing for Tatanka's arrival couldn't have been better. Fellow Native American Chief Jay Strongbow was nearing the end of his WWF career, and McMahon wanted to continue the tradition. Tatanka's full-blooded heritage was especially appealing. The WWF would soon take full advantage of that.

"Vince liked that I was truly Native American," Tatanka says. "They were wanting some-body who could do the Native American thing, and that was already my character. I was already wearing the loin-cloth. I was

"People could say 'Tatanka! Tatanka! Tatanka!' or 'Tanka! Tanka! Tanka!' instead of going 'Big Bear Running in the Woods! Big Bear Running in the Woods!'"

already doing what they wanted."

Originally, McMahon's new discovery simply debuted as "Chris Chavis." The WWF film crew traveled to the Lumbees' tribal land and shot vignettes (short promotional videos) featuring Tatanka in various outdoor settings with some of the tribal members serving as extras. Tatanka notched victories over Kato, Skinner, Barry Horowitz, and the Brooklyn Brawler, among others, in his early matches. Once a long-term contract was signed, McMahon wanted to take Tatanka's character a step further. He needed a new name. Tatanka took on the difficult task himself.

"With most native names, they have two or three full words in them," Tatanka explains. "Tatanka was basically the only native word that I could find that was just one word. People could say 'Tatanka! Tatanka! Tatanka!' or 'Tanka! Tanka! Tanka!' instead of going 'Big Bear Running in the Woods! Big Bear Running in the Woods!' The name Tatanka was also used in the movie *Dances with Wolves*, so it was a popular name at the time. It's actually a Lakota name that means 'Big Bull' or 'Big Buffalo.' Vince loved it."

Still not completely satisfied, however, McMahon came up with one last idea to usher Tatanka in with a bang. He asked Tatanka to cut his hair high and tight on the sides and let it grow out longer in the back. Then McMahon asked him to dye the hair on top of his head red. The red hair would come to represent Tatanka's tribal bloodline and eventually played an important part in one of Tatanka's most memorable feuds against Bam Bam Bigelow.

From the beginning of Tatanka's career with the WWF, he was groomed for a long, undefeated streak that would last two years. The other wrestlers quickly took notice. At that time it was rare for a newcomer to receive such an early push. "Instantly, they were doing a photo shoot of me for a poster," Tatanka recalls. "The Undertaker and all the boys were going, 'Whoa, look at this, already getting his own merchandise.'"

Two months after joining the WWF, Tatanka officially debuted with a feud against Rick "The Model" Martel, a seasoned veteran whose job was to help bring Tatanka along with some on-the-job training. With little hype, the two wrestlers suddenly found themselves meeting in semi-main event matches. Martel established himself as the heel by stealing Tatanka's ceremonial feather and spraying him in the face with a "can of arrogance." But Tatanka had already won the hearts of fans with his pre-match war dance, the occasional war cry, and his rare combination of speed, strength, and aerial maneuvers. Tatanka electrified audiences with his tomahawk chop from the top rope and his signature fall-away slam, affectionately known as the "Papoose to Go," the "Indian Deathdrop," or the "End of the Trail." Tatanka and Martel would battle for the next year, with high-profile fights

> "I did not enjoy being a heel, but I enjoyed that I was able to do it. . . . A lot of people can be babyfaces or heels, but to be able to do both good, there's only a few who can do that."

at *Wrestlemania VIII* in 1991 and *Survivor Series* in 1992, where the feud officially ended. Tatanka credits Martel for schooling him in the finer arts of wrestling and helping him learn the trade.

Next up for Tatanka was another year-long feud, this time with "The Beast from the East," Bam Bam Bigelow. As difficult as it is for Tatanka to pinpoint a favorite feud during his WWF days, this one seems to be the front-runner. Even Bigelow has been known to agree and has often said he misses working with Tatanka more than any other wrestler. Bigelow's character's blatant disrespect for Tatanka's heritage heated up the feud. While appearing at Madison Square Garden in New York, Tatanka remembers the building shaking throughout the entire match.

For the next three years, Tatanka would carry on feuds that each lasted one year, a rarity in the modern wrestling industry. His feuds with I.R.S. (Mike Rotunda), Yokozuna, and Lex Luger yielded some of the most memorable matches of the 1990s. Tatanka's heel turn, in which he joined Ted DiBiase's "Million Dollar Team" and turned on Luger, the "All-American," was the most intriguing time of Tatanka's WWF career—but not his most enjoyable. His personable nature made it difficult to portray someone he didn't want to be outside of the ring. Regardless, he took the assignment seriously and went for broke.

"I did not enjoy being a heel, but I enjoyed that I was able to do it," Tatanka says. "It's one thing to make that turn, but it's another thing to do it and make money. A lot of people can be babyfaces or heels, but to be able to do both good, there's only a few who can do that. 'Macho Man' Randy Savage and Hulk Hogan can do that. It's not that I'm special. I just watched the tapes of the great heels, and I believed that I could do it."

In 1996, Tatanka was forced to take two months off from wrestling to clear his name in a legal issue. He also realized he needed to take care of some family concerns that had developed due to his rigorous traveling schedule. Michelle Chavis, Tatanka's wife of four years, was fighting loneliness, and she wanted more of his time. "You can't run three hundred days a year and have balance in your life," Tatanka says. "My life wasn't falling apart. I had all of the material things I needed. I wasn't doing drugs or anything like that. But I didn't have any balance in my marriage or my personal life."

Since January of that year Tatanka had sensed God tugging on his heart. At the time, he was unaware of what was really happening or Who he was wrestling with. Tatanka had run from his spiritual calling from the day he accepted Christ as a teenager, but now, faced with court battles and family difficulties, he was forced to stop just long enough for God to get his attention. While back at home, he began attending Touch of God Ministries in St. Petersburg, where he rededicated his life to Christ. Tatanka realized God had a special plan for his life as an apostolic and prophetic evangelist—quite a weighty responsibility and unusual calling for a self-made wrestling star. Looking back on that time, Tatanka can now see that God's ultimate plan for his life was finally beginning to take shape.

"That's when everything started happening," Tatanka says. "It was my time for that seed that had been planted years earlier to be manifested."

Several weeks later he returned to reprise his role of Tatanka for one last run to close out 1996. The WWF was struggling financially, and World Championship Wrestling (WCW) was giving McMahon a run for his money, stealing much of his talent and television ratings in the process. Still acting as a heel, Tatanka was faced with the daunting task of helping make fan-favorites out of the new crop of babyfaces (good guys) who had recently arrived on the scene. This would result in more defeats and fewer victories. Even more of a challenge was the uncomfortable dynamic that his recent conversion had created.

By the wrestling industry's standards, Tatanka's lifestyle had already been considered pretty conservative compared to the wild partying that most of his colleagues indulged in every night. Even so, he admits to joining in the revelry at times. Now, with his newfound relationship with God, Tatanka was spending less time in the clubs and more time in his hotel room reading his Bible and spending time in prayer. He also made a stronger commitment to his wife's needs. Frequent phone calls back home to Michelle were at the top of his newly prioritized agenda.

"When I went back to wrestling, everything was different," Tatanka says. "The guys noticed something was different about me. They just wanted me to be the way I had always been. I stopped doing some of the stupid things I'd been doing with the guys. They didn't like that. It was different, but by then, God had already gotten hold of me."

For the next two and half years, Tatanka stayed completely away from wrestling. He even turned down a lucrative offer from Eric Bischoff to join WCW. Tatanka had put away the money he had earned in the ring and was able to spend time with his wife, as the couple searched out what God had planned for their future.

"That whole time I was totally spending and focusing my time on God," Tatanka says. "It was God's time to get hold of me and show me a reality that I didn't even understand. The calling that had been on my life since I was a teenager was coming to pass."

During his sabbatical, he and Michelle decided to start a family. In May of 1996, their daughter, Christiana Mariah, was born. Spiritually, physically, and emotionally rejuvenated,

"Every call that I've received in wrestling since I came back has not come as a result of me picking up the phone one time. . . . How have I done it? It's because God is with me."

Tatanka headed back to the ring, but this time as part of the independent circuit. Initially, he struggled to find work, as he was unable to use the name Tatanka. McMahon and the WWF owned the trademark, but by early 2000, McMahon had allowed it to expire. Tatanka was alerted to the name's availability, and he immediately took legal action to acquire it for himself. For Tatanka, getting his name back was yet another confirmation that God was working and enabling him to return to mainstream wrestling. Later that year, McMahon claimed ownership of the name and attempted to block promoters from using it in their advertising, but McMahon was unaware he had lost the rights earlier. Tatanka's appearances increased dramatically. He was now traveling all over the U.S. and abroad.

"Every call that I've received in wrestling since I came back has not come as a result of me picking up the phone one time," Tatanka says. "I've worked more than anyone on the independent circuit. I've been booked an average of thirteen days a month and as many as twenty-one days in a month. I've been blessed with nights when I sold between $3,500 and $4,500 in merchandise. How have I done it? It's because God is with me. These are signs of the things that are coming. I gave up wrestling for His call. God always brings back to you what you give up. He always gives you the desires of your heart. He's always going to bring them back for the right reasons."

Tatanka is careful not to take credit for any of his past or future successes. His motto used to be "Believe in yourself." He has since changed that motto to "Believe in God." As an "apostolic prophetic evangelist," Tatanka has no choice.

"Why me?" Tatanka asks. "Not because Chris Chavis is special, but it's because I've accepted the calling and I'm trying to do what He wants me to do. It means doing His will and putting away my life. It's hard to do. I'll be the first one to tell you, it's not easy. But with God's power and His grace, you'll go right through it. There is a price to pay if you want to be used by God mightily."

Many of Tatanka's exploits have not been widely publicized. The miracles and manifestations of God's power that he has witnessed have made him bold in sharing his faith, and his witness has affected a number of people in the wrestling business. Tatanka is responsible for numerous conversions to Christ by some of the industry's biggest names, but his influence doesn't stop there. Tatanka awaits the opening of the biggest door yet. It's an unseen reality that he expects to materialize at any moment.

"I will not be able to take glory in any of it. It will all be done by the hands of God and His Son, Jesus Christ."

"I believe God is going to raise me to the top of wrestling," Tatanka says with confidence. "He's going to bring forth someone who will honor Him . . . He's also going to bring the truth into the world of wrestling. People will be shocked by what is going to happen. There will be many people who will say, 'There's no way that company would shut down' or 'There's no way that company would ever fall.'"

According to Tatanka, his future involvement with the industry will focus on two purposes: to help clean up wrestling's tarnished image by creating a cleaner, more wholesome product, and to draw attention to the message of Christ. It's hard to argue with a man who's seen the dead brought back to life.

"Families will want to watch wrestling because it portrays a good image and a good hero overcoming a villain and overcoming evil," Tatanka says. "When you see this come to pass, you're going to realize that Chris Chavis has been walking with God and Chris Chavis has heard from God. More importantly, you're going to realize that everything that's happened in my career and everything that is going to happen was not done by my hands and not orchestrated by me. I will not be able to take glory in any of it. It will all be done by the hands of God and His Son, Jesus Christ."

TATANKA

TATANKA

FULL NAME: Chris Chavis

NICKNAMES: Tatanka, War Eagle, The Native American

BIRTHDATE: June 8, 1960

BIRTHPLACE: Pembroke, North Carolina

HOMETOWN: St. Petersburg, Florida

EDUCATION: Bethel High School, Hampton, Virginia; Undergraduate Studies at James Madison University

HEIGHT: 6'1"

WEIGHT: 275

FAMILY: Michelle (wife); Christiana (daughter)

PRO WRESTLING DEBUT: Defeated Joe Thunderstorm in Philadelphia, Pennsylvania (WWA)

PROMOTIONS: WWF, SAPW, WXL, UCW, Stampede Wrestling, JWA, WWA, CCW, FOW, USWA, ASWSA, ECWA, NEWF, UWFSA, WCWJ

TITLES HELD: SAPW Heavyweight, USWA Heavyweight; ASWSA South American Heavyweight; 1990 Pro Wrestling Illustrated Rookie of the Year

FINISHING MOVES: Tomahawk chop off the top rope; Fall away slam (a.k.a. Papoose To Go, Indian Deathdrop, End of the Trail)

BEST FEUDS: vs. Bam Bam Bigelow; vs. Rick Martel; vs. J.R.S.; vs. Yokozuna; vs. Lex Luger

WORST INJURY: Dislocated kneecap vs. the Undertaker in Nassau, NY; strained knee ligaments

THE MILLION
DOLLAR MAN
CHAPTER 2

THE MILLION DOLLAR MAN
CHAPTER 2

Ted DiBiase's eyes are glued to his laptop computer screen. As he sits at a small wooden desk in a hotel room, his 6-foot 4-inch, 280-pound frame overwhelms a chair that seems unsure of its ability to hold a man of that size. The modest room contains a king-sized bed and a couch, but pales in comparison to the five-star establishments DiBiase frequented while at the height of his career with the World Wrestling Federation (WWF). Leaning closer to the computer screen, he reads to himself for a while, then whispers some of the text and stops.

"This is blowing me away," he says.

DiBiase is reading an e-mail from a thirty-five-year-old woman who used to watch him wrestle with Georgia Championship Wrestling during the early 1980s. She shares her sad story of growing up without a mother and enduring abuse from her father. Watching professional wrestling on television was one of her favorite means of escaping reality. She says DiBiase was her hero, a "silent mentor" in her life.

DiBiase reads some of the letter aloud: "I felt a need to write to you and tell you that even though we may not know one another personally, that in some strange way you saved my life while I was growing up and have touched it in ways that you are unaware of."

The e-mail is one of hundreds that DiBiase receives each day through his Web site (*www.milliondollarman.com*), and although he tries to answer them all, he's not always successful. This particular e-mail is especially compelling. "Things like that, I've got to answer," he says.

DiBiase can relate to people with family problems. He grew up around distrust, misfortune, and tragedy. DiBiase doesn't talk a lot about his birth father. There's not much to say. He was just a toddler when his mother's second husband walked away. Born in Miami, Florida, Ted and his older brother and mother were left to fend for themselves. That's when Mike DiBiase stepped into the picture. Ted was five years old when his mother finally found happiness with the professional wrestler known as "Iron Mike." He was not only well-respected throughout the professional wrestling industry, but he also had been a national collegiate amateur champion at the University of Nebraska.

"Mike DiBiase became my dad," DiBiase says. "He adopted me, changed my name, and more importantly loved me as his own son. I really looked up to and admired this man. It meant a lot to me to please him. So I wanted to be an athlete."

For ten years, DiBiase received an education on the wrestling business by watching his stepfather like a hawk. "Growing up in the wrestling business was like growing up in the army," DiBiase explains. "You wouldn't stay in any one place too long and overexpose yourself. You would leave and come back. That's how I grew up." Arizona, Texas, and Nebraska were familiar spots for the DiBiase clan.

The family also spent an extended amount of time in Omaha, Nebraska, where Ted attended middle school. For his freshman year of high school, he attended Creighton Prep, an all-boys

"Growing up in the wrestling business was like growing up in the army."

Catholic school known for its strong athletic program. But just as DiBiase was getting excited about his future there, the wrestling bug struck again, and the family moved to Texas during the summer of 1969.

It was July 2, 1969, and the U.S. was days away from triumphantly landing on the moon. But for DiBiase, what happened that day would overshadow the moon walk. DiBiase and his brother were already tucked away in bed when the phone call came. Iron Mike had suffered a heart attack during a match and died in the ring. "That changed my life forever," DiBiase says.

DiBiase's mother slipped into a deep depression and turned to alcohol for comfort. Unable to deal with the pressure of losing a third husband and caring for two teenage boys, she sent DiBiase off to southern Arizona to live with his grandparents in the small town of Wilcox. He finished high school there, and his outstanding prowess at football earned him a scholarship to the University of Arizona. But DiBiase changed his mind and decided to attend West Texas State, a smaller school just south of Amarillo. It was closer to the legendary wrestling Funk family, from whom he hoped to learn more about the profession.

"In the back of my mind I thought it might not be football, it might be wrestling," DiBiase says. "I might not be good enough for the NFL."

Each summer, DiBiase spent time with Dory Funk Sr. and his sons, Dory Jr. and Terry, learning the ropes through the Amarillo territory that they ran. At the young age of twenty, DiBiase got married, and the responsibility quickly overwhelmed him. The marriage would last only a short while. Wrestling was DiBiase's true love and would eventually cost him more than his first marriage.

After his junior year at West Texas State, he decided to spend the summer working for Mid-South Wrestling with promoter Cowboy Bill Watts. The NCAA had just passed a ruling that allowed an athlete to complete professionally in one sport while maintaining amateur status in another. Watts was legendary for requiring his wrestlers to endure grueling work schedules and less-than-reasonable travel plans. DiBiase covered every inch of Mississippi, Louisiana, and Arkansas that summer, but it was the best learning process he could ever go through.

This first experience in the ring left DiBiase wanting more. He never did make it back to West Texas State. "I was going to wrestle for the summer and go back to school," DiBiase says. "I got a taste of being on the road and a good taste of the business, and I was doing well. I was learning the business. I was a year away from earning my degree, and I walked away. I still regret that."

DiBiase spent nine months in New York and claimed the WWWF North American title. . . . His last match in New York was against a young Hulk Hogan.

The first Mid-South experience lasted nearly two years and included a U.S. Tag Team title with Dick Murdoch and a North American heavyweight championship. Still at an early point in his career, DiBiase was achieving main event status.

DiBiase spent parts of 1977 and 1978 in the Kansas City territory before landing back in Amarillo for a one-year run. While wrestling in St. Louis a year earlier, DiBiase caught the eye of Vince McMahon Sr., who brought him to New York to work the World Wide Wrestling Federation (WWWF). He spent the next nine months competing for attention with the likes of Superstar Billy Graham and Bruno Sammartino.

"Although they liked me and they liked my work, [Billy and Bruno] had become big stars, and all of a sudden that's where the image of a wrestler became his body," DiBiase says. "I didn't have a great body. My ability was that I could produce in the ring and I could talk on the microphone."

DiBiase spent nine months in New York and claimed the WWWF North American title for the bulk of his time there. His last match in New York was against a young Hulk Hogan. It was Hogan's first match ever in Madison Square Garden, and the two had become friends. DiBiase always looked out for Hogan, and the rising star never forgot that. "I owe you one, buddy," Hogan once told DiBiase.

And Hogan would keep his word.

Over the next eight years, DiBiase would spend a great deal of time in and out of the Mid-South promotion. He loved working for Watts, and his own celebrity status had grown to outrageous proportions in certain parts of the country. At one point, he was voted the most popular athlete in the state of Louisiana—ahead of the entire New Orleans Saints football team. DiBiase's feud with the Junkyard Dog during the 1980s is still considered one of the classic battles of that decade. "Even today I have fans who come up to me, and they remember Mid-South Wrestling," DiBiase says.

When not with Mid-South, DiBiase traveled the National Wrestling Alliance (NWA) recognized circuits, where he was told he was being groomed to be the next NWA World Champion. The plan was to move the championship around among three athletes, Dusty Rhodes, Ric Flair, and DiBiase. But somehow, only Rhodes and Flair ever saw the belt around their waists.

It was late 1980 when DiBiase made his next big career change. He left Mid-South once again, this time for Atlanta and Georgia Championship Wrestling. Jimmy Crockett was building a mini-empire in the South, and with the help of Ted Turner's cable networks, many of the wrestlers were becoming household names. The recently divorced DiBiase was finally able to reduce his traveling to short trips and make time for his personal life. A few months after making the change, he met his future wife, Melanie.

"When I fell in love with Melanie, I fell in love with a Christian girl," DiBiase says. "Melanie at the time was not living a particularly Christian life. She was having fun, and she was going to college. She helped me move to Baton Rouge, Louisiana, where I went to work for Mid-South again."

But DiBiase was lonely, and his time away from Melanie made

him realize he was in love with her. A few weeks after moving to Baton Rouge, he visited her in Georgia and made the pitch.

"I can't live without you," DiBiase pined.

It wasn't a marriage proposal, but a plea for Melanie to move to Baton Rouge and live with him there. DiBiase had been raised Roman Catholic but had long ago stopped attending church. Melanie started attending a Bible study. Around the same time, DiBiase met Hal Santos, the owner of a gym where he worked out. Santos, a pastor, asked DiBiase why he was living with Melanie when the two were not married. He encouraged DiBiase to repent of his sin and either move out or get married. The couple chose the latter, and on New Year's Eve 1981, DiBiase and Melanie were wed.

For the next several years, DiBiase went through the motions. He wanted his second marriage to succeed, but he admittedly wanted a successful wrestling career even more. For the next six years, the couple bounced around from Louisiana with Mid-South back to Atlanta for Georgia Championship Wrestling, then to Mississippi where the couple settled down permanently after accepting another offer to work for Watts. Singles titles and tag team championships followed DiBiase everywhere he went. Trying to keep God at the center of his life, DiBiase made two separate personal commitments to Christ and was baptized, but the road provided many distractions that impeded his spiritual growth.

"I walked the aisle and I said all of the right things, but I didn't surrender," DiBiase says. "I recognized that Jesus was the Son of God, and I believed it. I recognized that I must have that relationship. I knew that I had it in a childlike way as a kid, and I wanted it again. I wanted my marriage to be good, but I had an idol in my life: wrestling. I wanted to be a star. I wanted God on my terms. When I was on the road, I didn't get up on Sundays and go look for a church service. I didn't turn on the television and look for a church service. I didn't read my Bible every day. I gave lip service. I did those things when it happened to be convenient."

"I walked the aisle and I said all of the right things, but I didn't surrender. I recognized that Jesus was the Son of God, and I believed it. . . . but I had an idol in my life: wrestling. I wanted to be a star. I wanted God on my terms."

From 1985 to 1987, professional wrestling took the country by storm. Vince McMahon Jr. was in control of the WWF, and the wrestling world watched in awe at the huge numbers generated by *Wrestlemania I, II,* and *III.* The third installment took place in March of 1987 and set an indoor attendance record at the Superdome in New Orleans, with a main event that featured Hulk Hogan versus Andre the Giant. Shortly after, DiBiase received an unexpected call from McMahon himself. He wanted a one-on-one meeting in New York. DiBiase remembers the conversation well.

"I've got an idea, and I've got to have the right guy to do this," McMahon said. "I think, Ted, you're the guy to pull it off. You interview well. You're well spoken. You carry yourself well. You're the arrogant type of heel, and that's what I want. You know how wrestling is. Everything's been done, and it's unique when something comes along that hasn't been done. This character has never been done. But I can't tell you what it is unless you agree to come on board."

DiBiase thought about it for the next few days. He consulted his old friend Terry Funk, who was more like a big brother. "If Vince McMahon has an idea for you that's his own idea, he's going to make sure it works," Funk advised. "Do it!"

After calling McMahon to accept his offer, DiBiase was told to come back to New York, where the master plan would be revealed. Melanie accompanied him, and the two were treated to a stay at the Helmsley Palace. They ate in the best restaurants and rode in a limousine between destinations. DiBiase ended up in McMahon's office, where he and McMahon were joined by WWF executive and legendary wrestler Pat Patterson. Sitting across from the shrewd businessman, DiBiase could feel the passionate fire in McMahon's coal-black eyes.

"We're going to make you the 'Million Dollar Man,'" McMahon emphatically told DiBiase. "You are going to live the lifestyle. Everywhere you go, you're going to be chauffeured. I'll expect you to stay in the finest hotels. You'll dress the part. You'll look the part. Anywhere you're in public, you will be the Million Dollar Man."

McMahon continued to detail his plan for DiBiase's immediate future. DiBiase was stunned. When McMahon was called away to take an important phone call in another room, Patterson took over where his boss had left off.

"Ted, if Vince could put on the tights and climb in the ring, he'd be the Million Dollar Man," Patterson explained. "You've got to do this, because you will be living out Vince's role."

"We're going to make you the 'Million Dollar Man.' . . . You are going to live the lifestyle. Everywhere you go, you're going to be chauffeured. . . . You'll dress the part. You'll look the part. Anywhere you're in public, you will be the Million Dollar Man."

When DiBiase left the meeting, he was in a state of shock. Melanie had been patiently waiting for her husband and was greeted by an unusual request.

"Pinch me," DiBiase said. "This isn't real. This isn't happening to me."

But over the next several weeks, the Million Dollar Man became reality. The WWF taped several vignettes to prepare the way. DiBiase's character was a wealthy man who bought everything he wanted. He was portrayed as heartless and cold, a role DiBiase had performed well as a classic heel throughout much of his career. One especially memorable bit featured DiBiase offering a young boy the chance to win a large sum of money if he could dribble a basketball ten consecutive times without error. The boy easily reached nine before DiBiase knocked the ball away and ruthlessly denied him the prize.

When the Million Dollar Man finally debuted in the WWF, he was a huge hit. The fans loved to hate his arrogant character. Right away, he was inserted into the World Heavyweight title picture. After DiBiase's unsuccessful attempts at securing the belt, a clever storyline had him "buying" the title from Andre the Giant. DiBiase was never officially recognized as the champion, so the title was vacated and a tournament was held to determine the rightful owner. That led to DiBiase's first appearance at a major pay-per-view event, *Wrestlemania IV*. But he lost in the finals to Randy "Macho Man" Savage and never got much closer. His 1988 "King of the Ring" title was but one isolated singles highlight.

For the next five years, DiBiase was mostly tied up in the tag team division with Mike Rotundo (a.k.a. Irwin R. Schyster). The duo won three tag titles between February 1992 and June 1993. But while DiBiase was on top of the wrestling world, his "Million Dollar Man" lifestyle was taking a toll on his spiritual life, which in turn adversely affected his marriage. His pastor and good friend

Hal Santos had warned him that he needed to stay accountable and continue growing through prayer, Bible reading, and daily devotions, because Satan was going to attack his greatest weaknesses. For DiBiase, his pride and ego had led him down a near-destructive path.

"I didn't do that [follow Santos' guidance]," DiBiase admits. "I started living that life to where I was having a good time, and I was making money, and I was getting all of those things I thought I wanted. But I wasn't being the spiritual leader of my family, and I wasn't the husband and father I should have been. I loved them, but the idol in my life was the business. I started to rationalize all of the things I was doing on the road."

It was March 1992, and DiBiase had just taken part in *Wrestlemania VIII*, his fifth consecutive appearance in wrestling's grandest spectacle. He had been out all night partying and failed to call home. DiBiase flew to Chicago, where he checked into another hotel and finally made the call to a wife that he describes as "livid." She had discovered the truth about some of DiBiase's road habits.

"You'd better start talking and you'd better tell the truth, because I know the truth," Melanie told her husband. "First lie that comes out of your mouth, it's over."

"I don't want to talk about this on the phone," DiBiase replied. "I'll be on the next plane home."

"No you won't," she said. "You don't live here anymore."

Click.

DiBiase was stunned. His heart sank as his wife's voice was reduced to a dial tone. But confusion quickly turned to clarity. For the first time in his life, he knew it was time for some serious changes. The first step was finding a way to repair the breach in his marriage. DiBiase called Santos, who flew to Chicago and spent the evening counseling him. The wrestler then begrudgingly flew to Europe for a mandatory three-day tour. Upon his return, Santos arranged for DiBiase and Melanie to meet in St. Louis. She wanted to see her husband face-to-face.

"That was the longest plane ride and the longest car ride of my life," DiBiase says. "I asked Hal, 'What do I do?' Basically he was saying I had to choose whom I was going to serve. So before I walked in that door, I prayed a little prayer and asked God to forgive me. All my wrestling friends told me to lie, but I told the truth, the whole miserable truth. That was the hardest thing I ever did."

Not sure if their marriage would withstand the blow, DiBiase and Melanie continued to work through their problems with Santos' help. They stayed in St. Louis for a few days, where they attended a youth rally for more than three thousand teenagers. DiBiase remembers little about the preacher, much less the sermon he preached. But it didn't take long for DiBiase to understand why he was in such strange surroundings.

"I was there because God wanted to deal with my ego," DiBiase says. "God was asking me, 'Are you willing to humble yourself?' That preacher gave the altar call, and I got out of my chair, and I beat every kid to the front. I got on my knees, and I got on my face, and I cried like a baby. I finally realized that the key word is 'surrender.'"

The next two years brought a series of trials by fire to DiBiase's marriage. While still wrestling for the WWF, he worked hard to keep his new commitment to Melanie. But the challenges were not limited to the home. DiBiase's career was in peril as well. His career as an active wrestler came to a sudden halt when he injured two cervical disks in his neck. DiBiase was reduced to a managerial role for the likes of Andre the Giant and Steve Austin. His career with the WWF was nearing its end.

DiBiase's next stop was World Championship Wrestling, where he became involved in one of the hottest angles in wrestling history.

DiBiase's next stop was World Championship Wrestling, where he became involved in one of the hottest angles in wrestling history. Just as the New World Order (NWO) was staking its claim with Hulk Hogan, Kevin Nash, and Scott Hall, WCW president Eric Bischoff brought DiBiase in to portray a character similar to the Million Dollar Man. Dubbed "Trillionaire Ted" by Hogan, DiBiase became the man bankrolling the NWO's operation.

Things changed quickly, however, as Bischoff surprised everyone by announcing that he was the true leader of the NWO. Suddenly, DiBiase's position was diminished. No longer satisfied with being Hogan's belt-bearer, DiBiase approached Bischoff about a change. He was sent home until a new role could be created.

When WCW finally called on DiBiase, he was brought back to manage the Steiner brothers in what he considered a nonsensical move. It didn't last long. In May 1999, both Steiners were injured, and once again DiBiase was put on the shelf. He served as a technical adviser for a video game project and reported for WCW Motor Sports but otherwise was never used by WCW again in a wrestling-related event.

At that point in DiBiase's life, he didn't care anymore. He was already seeing that his future was in the ministry. DiBiase had been speaking in churches and had written his autobiography, *Every Man Has a Price.* Appearances on *The 700 Club* and the Trinity Broadcasting Network (TBN) further solidified the move. "When I say there's a call on my life by God, a lot of people don't understand what that means," DiBiase says. "But in fact, that's what I believe. I believe that call has been on my life since I was a kid, but for too long I ignored it."

MILLION DOLLAR MAN

DiBiase stopped ignoring his family as well. His spiritual growth over the previous seven years was reaping benefits at home with Melanie and their son, Teddy. According to DiBiase, his marriage is stronger and more intimate than ever before. In 1999, DiBiase started Heart of David Ministries and also lent his name to WXO Wrestling, a promotion aimed at a more family-friendly presentation. The WXO shut down its operation in 2000, but DiBiase has hopes of starting his own wrestling promotion as a ministry. His personal ministry has had a major impact on several star wrestlers. Sting, Chris Jericho, Eddie Guerrero, Marcus Bagwell, and Scott Hall have all had encounters with DiBiase that left a lasting impression.

But perhaps DiBiase's heart is burdened most for the man who gave him his biggest break: Vince McMahon Jr. Although they have not spoken since the Million Dollar Man's departure from the WWF, DiBiase credits McMahon with making him who he is today—but he also blames him for wrestling's moral downfall. DiBiase, usually calm and laid back, jumps to the edge of his seat and raises his voice a decibel or two when he talks about the current state of wrestling. But he is equally passionate about the debt he owes McMahon and even more so concerning the condition of his soul.

"I've been criticized for using the character that Vince McMahon built for me to blast his company," DiBiase says. "People accuse me of biting the hand that fed me. But I've always given credit to Vince, and I'll always be grateful to him for the best years of my career. That doesn't mean that I should stand by idly and watch them destroy our business and make it into something that it shouldn't be. If I had a chance to talk to Vince McMahon today, I would tell him that I pray for him, because I do. I pray for him. I pray for his family. I pray for the World Wrestling Federation and all of the guys in it. And I pray that one day God will open up their eyes."

TED DiBiASE

FULL NAME: Theodore Marvin DiBiase

WRESTLING NICKNAMES: The Million Dollar Man; Trillionaire Ted

PERSONAL NICKNAMES: Dibo; Diber

BIRTHDATE: January 18, 1954

BIRTHPLACE: Miami, Florida

HOMETOWN: Clinton, Mississippi

EDUCATION: Undergraduate Studies at West Texas State

HEIGHT: 6'4"

WEIGHT: 280

FAMILY: Melanie (wife); Teddy (son)

PRO WRESTLING DEBUT: June 1975

FIRST MATCH: Lost to Danny Hodge

PROMOTIONS: Mid-South, Georgia Championship Wrestling, WCW, WWF, All Japan Pro Wrestling, Tri-States, Amarillo Territory, NWA, UWF, WXO Wrestling

TITLES HELD: Mid-South Tag Team, Mid-South North American Heavyweight (5x), Missouri Central States Champion (2x), Missouri Central States Heavyweight (2x), Amarillo International, Western States Tag Team, Western States Tag Team, WWWF North American, Georgia National Tag Team (2x), Mid-South Tag Team (4x), All-Japan United National Champion, Georgia National Heavyweight (2x), Texas All-Star USA Champion, UWF Tag Team, All-Japan PWF Tag Team (2x), WWF World Tag Team (3x), All-Japan Unified Tag Team, All-Japan Real World Tag Team Tournament Champion, WWF King of the Ring Champion

FINISHING MOVES: Figure-four leg lock; Sleeper hold; Million Dollar Dream

FAVORITE FEUD: vs. Junkyard Dog

WORST INJURY: Career-ending injury to two cervical discs in neck

STiNG
CHAPTER 3

STING

CHAPTER 3

Silence, if but for the briefest of moments, overcomes Panama Beach, Florida. Then, with the flash of strobe-induced lightning, the crowd erupts with great anticipation. The Jumbotron broadcasts a chaotic array of images as Metallica's "Seek and Destroy" serves as the soundtrack. Finally, a man emerges to a hero's welcome, clearly the most boisterous cheer of the evening. His full-body black tights are engulfed by his trademark scorpion logo. His face is painted white with black coloring on his eyes and mouth. Tonight has been dubbed "Night of Champions" on *Monday Nitro*, and it seems only fitting that Sting, often called the franchise of World Championship Wrestling (WCW), should close out the show in a classic match against his longtime foe, Ric "The Nature Boy" Flair.

The seasoned veterans stare each other down, and the dance begins. They lock arms briefly before Sting gains the upper hand. Flair fights back with a series of painful chops that redden Sting's chest. There's a burst of energy, and suddenly Sting takes Flair to the mat with a hip toss. Before he can regain his balance, Sting takes him back down with a drop kick. Flair leaves the ring to assess the situation. Sting cups his hands to his mouth and lets loose with a resounding "Owwwww!"

"Stinger! Stinger! Stinger!" the crowd responds with chants of approval.

Flair reenters the ring, and the two exchange smiles. There is a great deal of mutual respect between these seasoned grapplers. For the next fifteen minutes, the ebb and flow changes, with each man alternately taking control of the momentum. Finally, after breaking free from Flair's infamous "figure four leg lock," Sting pounds Flair to the ground, then hoists his body into a sitting position on the top rope of the ring's corner turnbuckle. Sting tosses Flair from the top rope to the mat, allowing him to apply his own signature hold, the "Scorpion Deathlock." Flair, like most victims, taps out, giving the painted one the victory. Helping his defeated opponent off the mat, Sting heartily embraces Flair. The two shake hands and embrace once again as the crowd cheers.

It wasn't the most epic battle between the two, but it may have been the most historic. This meeting between Sting and Flair on March 26, 2001, would be the last in front of a Turner Network Television (TNT) audience. WCW would never be the same. It was now owned by World Wrestling Federation (WWF) owner Vince McMahon Jr., and the future remained unclear for WCW, its employees, and especially Sting, or Steve Borden, as his family and friends know him. With chunks of face paint smeared away, Sting's eyes are revealed as he looks to the screen awaiting, if not dreading, the inevitable announcement from McMahon. The events that have transpired over the past forty-eight hours are like nothing he's seen in his storied career.

Sting has spent fifteen years making his name as someone else, in a wrestling ring, behind a painted-on mask, underneath a variety of made-to-order costumes. On the streets, some people recognize him, but many don't. That's the beauty of being Sting. Unlike most wrestlers of his era who started in their late teens and early twenties, Sting didn't entertain thoughts of professional wrestling until the

Sting has spent fifteen years making his name as someone else, in a wrestling ring, behind a painted on mask, underneath a variety of made-to-order costumes.

age of twenty-six. He lacked the strong wrestling tradition in his family that had helped such notables as the Harts, the Von Erichs, and the Guerreros. No, Sting would instead take an uncharted path to wrestling stardom.

Born March 20, 1959, in Omaha, Nebraska, Sting was the first sibling of four. Two years later, younger brother Jeff joined the Borden family, and the two became inseparable as they shared similar goals and dreams over the next twenty-one years. The

Borden family eventually left the Midwest for the suburbs of Los Angeles. The family continued to grow, with the addition of younger sister Kelley and youngest brother Mark. Once Steve and Jeff were old enough to live on their own, the rowdy duo moved into a house that they would share for about five years. They regularly hosted parties for their friends.

But the craziness abruptly ended in 1983 when Jeff, at the age of twenty-one, had a life-changing experience. While attending a church Easter pageant with his girlfriend (and soon to be wife), Lori, Jeff accepted Christ. Things changed quickly for the previously inseparable brothers. They moved out on their own, and both got married. Jeff went on to a successful career with a technical firm, while Steve continued his involvement in athletics. He spent time playing basketball for College of the Canyons before moving into the health and fitness industry. As a disciplined bodybuilder, he found work as a private trainer and eventually became a co-owner of various workout facilities. Sting would later go on to open gyms in Atlanta with fellow wrestling superstar Lex Luger.

While balancing multiple jobs as a bouncer and a bartender, Sting excelled as a bodybuilder, and he eventually became a professional competitor. He reached the peak of his short-lived career in 1984 when he came within one point of qualifying for the Mr. USA finals. It was just one year later when Sting's life took an unexpected turn. While working at Gold's Gym in Venice Beach, California, he was approached by an out-of-place man on a mission.

"Somebody came in one day with three big guys," Sting recalls. "This little manager guy named Rick Bassman was looking for a fourth member of his wrestling team. It took some time, but he finally talked me into doing it, and that's how it all started."

In the world of wrestling, however, Sting was a complete novice. Though a natural athlete with a charismatic personality to match, he didn't quite catch the vibe until he saw his first major wrestling show, which featured a much younger and increasingly popular Hulk Hogan, the only professional wrestler Sting had even heard of at that point. He then began a rigorous training program with Bassman and Red Bastien, training alongside another new prospect, Jim Hellwig. The pair joined up with Mark Miller and Garland Donohoe to form Power Team USA. Sting took on the name "Flash," and Hellwig became "Justice."

Just a few months into its alliance, Power Team USA split up, but Sting and Hellwig stayed together and formed the Freedom Fighters. The pair moved to Nashville, Tennessee, where they worked for Jerry Jarrett's Mid-Southern Wrestling promotions. They didn't last long. Three months later, not only had they been buried in the booking sheets, but also they killed their gimmick. Sting and Hellwig became heels and formed the Blade Runners. Now, the former Steve Borden officially became Sting, and Hellwig became "Rock." Looking for greener pastures, the Blade Runners went to work for Cowboy Watts and the Mid-South promotion, which eventually became the Universal Wrestling Federation (UWF). Almost as soon as they arrived, Hellwig split from Sting and left the promotion. He eventually moved on to become an international star as The Ultimate Warrior in the WWF and briefly with WCW. Over the next year, Sting spent much of his time in cities such as Nashville, Tulsa, Oklahoma, and Alexandria, Louisiana, teaming up with the likes of Eddie Gilbert and Rick Steiner in a wrestling stable known as "Hot Stuff." He won a pair of tag team titles, one each with Gilbert and Steiner.

By 1987, the UWF was joining forces with the National Wrestling Alliance (NWA) on a regular basis. The NWA was second only to the WWF in popularity, and that helped Sting gain more notoriety with every appearance. Sting's bleach blond, crew-cut hairstyle and glittery costumes were matched by face paint that coordinated with the bright colors featured in his ring attire. To further solidify the character, Sting trademarked his name, a trademark he still owns, contrary to the popular belief that rock star and former Police front man Gordon Sumner—also known as Sting—has official rights to the name.

The first signs of a lengthy rivalry between Sting and Ric Flair developed in 1988. Since Sting was already a fan favorite, it made sense to pit him against Flair, the veteran heel. Several matches ensued, but the standard was set at the first *Clash of the Champions* where the two fought to a grueling draw after forty-five minutes. *WrestleWar '90* was the venue for their next confrontation, but this time, Sting lost the match and in the process tore the tendon in his right patella. Sting made a quick recovery and five months later took the World Heavyweight title from Flair at the *Great American Bash*. It would be the first of seven title reigns for Sting.

By this time, Jim Crockett, the owner of NWA affiliated Mid-Atlantic Championship Wrestling, had already sold his promotion to Ted Turner. It was now called World Championship Wrestling. Sting would ultimately be tabbed the franchise player. For the bet-ter part of the '90s, he lit up the arenas in memorable feuds against the likes of Flair, Lex Luger, Rick Rude, Sid Vicious, Vader, Nikita Koloff, Jake Roberts, and Cactus Jack (a.k.a. Mick Foley). He

Sting made a quick recovery and five months later took the World Heavyweight title from Flair at the *Great American Bash*. It would be the first of seven title reigns for Sting.

even defeated "Stunning" Steve Austin for the WCW U.S. title long before Austin's "Stone Cold" days.

By 1996, things were starting to heat up for WCW. Sting was arguably the most popular wrestler in the federation, rivaled only by the likes of Flair, Hulk Hogan, and Randy Savage. But what Eric Bischoff had planned for the next several months would help Sting's popularity skyrocket to another level. The television show *Nitro* was only a year old, but already it was offering some serious competition to its WWF counterpart, *Raw Is War.* In fact, Bischoff was aiming squarely at McMahon, hoping to pull off a major ratings upset. In June, Scott Hall and Kevin Nash made their debut and were portrayed as "The Outsiders" attempting to take over WCW. The former WWF stars would show up randomly and wreak havoc with surprise attacks against anyone who stood in their way. Early on, Sting was the natural choice to lead WCW's retaliation in this now legendary feud.

Later that summer, at the *Bash at the Beach* pay-per-view, Sting, Luger, and Savage took on the Outsiders and a mystery partner. The stage for Sting's meteoric rise was being set as he accidentally knocked out Luger with an errant "Stinger Splash." This would later help create distrust between Sting and his fellow WCW compatriots. But an even bigger swerve occurred when Hogan was revealed as the mystery partner, and he became a heel for the first time in his illustrious career. Hogan donned the new name of "Hollywood" and became known as the leader of the New World Order (NWO).

For the next year, Sting never spoke on camera but instead maintained the role of a vigilante with a cool wrath. He became the most talked-about figure in wrestling, as he lurked from the rafters, charged through the stands, or ripped through the bottom of the wrestling ring. No matter what the scenario, the result was always the same: a quick surprise entrance and an equally quick and mysterious exit. His most famous stunts took place when he would randomly rappel from arena ceilings. At an outdoor event,

STING

he stunned the crowd by dropping hundreds of feet from a helicopter. Sting's look was changing as well. He let his hair grow out and ditched the peroxide for his natural brown hair color. Black became the new theme for his attire, and his face changed to completely white with blackened eyes and lips. He looked less like the surfer Sting of old.

Toward the end of Sting's one-year wrestling sabbatical, the stage was set for a monumental confrontation between Sting and "Hollywood" Hulk Hogan. The two superstars would face off at the *Starrcade* pay-

"Everything on the surface seemed to be great, but for fourteen years, being a wrestler . . . took its toll . . . At one point, J felt like J was losing my family."

per-view on December 28, 1997. It was Sting's first match in a year, which showed early on. In what appeared to be a victory for Hogan, a third legend, Bret Hart, protested the decision, replaced the referee, and continued the match that Sting ultimately won to claim the heavyweight title.

While Sting was at the height of his career, he was also experiencing personal challenges. WCW required several days each month for television events, house shows, and pay-per-view broadcasts, not to mention the numerous personal appearances that his celebrity status demanded. Sting's new image had vaulted his wrestling career to its highest point; as a result, Sting was spending more time on the road and less time at home.

"Everything on the surface seemed to be great," Sting says. "But for fourteen years, being a wrestler and being away from my family, my wife, and my children, more than I wanted to be, took its toll on my family. We went through some really rough times. At one point, I felt like I was losing my family."

Between 1996 and 1998, Sting had several encounters that would begin reshaping his life. While Jeff occasionally shared Christ with his brother from a distance and constantly prayed for him, three of Sting's colleagues played important roles in his spiritual awakening. Marcus "Buff" Bagwell and Marc Mero, better known at the time as Johnny B. Badd, each had several one-on-one conversations with Borden about the Christian faith. Retired wrestler Ted DiBiase was especially influential in those early times; his beliefs were common knowledge among the entire WCW staff. On occasion, Sting would strike up a conversation with DiBiase, and invariably the "God thing" would creep into the dialogue. But DiBiase's best opportunities to share his faith with Sting developed when his mother sent him a copy of DiBiase's autobiography, *Every Man Has a Price.*

"Where it all came together, where I really realized I had an opportunity to witness to [Steve], came about by him reading my book," DiBiase says. "He told me that he had never read a book cover to cover without putting it down. There were so many similarities that he identified with."

For Sting, the timing was strangely ironic. Many of the things DiBiase conveyed in his book directly correlated to the struggles Sting was experiencing in his marriage and his career. "I shared with Steve that it wasn't an accident," DiBiase says. "I told him it was indicative of the way God speaks to people. I said, 'God's dealing with you, buddy. He's talking to your heart.' So on a weekly basis, I just started to gently say to him, 'Hey, Stinger, how's it going, buddy?' And he knew what I meant."

"I felt all of a sudden that the Spirit was there. I felt forgiven, cleansed, and it was an incredible experience. I accepted Jesus Christ into my life, and it was long overdue."

DiBiase had shared Sting's story with a few close friends in the ministry, including Simeon Nix, a church music director from Brandon, Florida. Now the pastor of Bell Shoals Baptist Church, Nix and some colleagues had a chance meeting with Sting at an Orlando hotel when WCW was in town for a big event. As the conversation came to a close, the minister made a bold move that would stay with Sting for months.

"If you died today, do you know where you'd go?" Nix asked.

Shocked, Sting just stood there, not knowing how to respond. He was stumped and had no answer to Nix's question about where he would spend eternity.

"Think about it," Nix said, breaking the uncomfortable silence.

"Yeah, I will," Sting sheepishly replied.

"If you like, we could pray right now," Nix offered.

Sting was unprepared for what took place next, right in the middle of a busy hotel lobby. Nix and his friends placed their hands on the wrestling star and began to pray for him out loud. Sting tensed up, his eyes shifting from side to side, saying his own silent prayer in the hopes that no one would recognize him and wonder what was happening. "People were walking by, and I was sweating bullets," Sting recalls. "I was nervous. I was embarrassed."

Shortly after, Sting attended a Promise Keepers event in the Los Angeles Coliseum, where he stepped forward, along with many others of the 40,000 men in attendance, and recited the sinner's prayer—one of his many proclamations of repentance that missed the mark. But that all changed in August of 1998. "I felt all of a sudden that the Spirit was there," Sting says. "I felt forgiven, cleansed, and it was an incredible experience. I accepted Jesus Christ into my life, and it was long overdue. It should have been a long time ago."

Sting credits the prayers and support of Jeff and the rest of his family back home in California for the massive changes in his life. "I could not have done it without Jeff," Sting says. "It took me getting saved to realize just how important my brother is to me. Words can never describe how he was throughout this whole process. He is a very wise man. I don't know if I've ever met a man who's wiser than him."

Just prior to Sting's conversion, his family had moved back to their hometown. It was a harrowing task trying to convince his wife, Sue, that the trek back West was in the family's best interest. They had settled into a comfortable life in the Atlanta area, and it made little sense to relocate. They had both vowed to never return to their hometown—along one of Southern California's beaches, perhaps—but not to their hometown.

"God did impress upon me to leave Georgia and move back to California," Sting says. "I just kept telling my wife that I felt like I needed my family's influence, for our kids and for us. She was dumbfounded. To pull her out of there and both of my boys was kind of a rough thing. But God was working on me, and I persisted. Finally, Sue agreed to move back home."

While still in Georgia, Sting had made a habit of pulling into the parking lots of abandoned schools, old buildings, and empty churches. Whenever his wife was with him, she would ask what he was doing. Sting said he had been thinking about buying such a property and moving his brother there to start a church and school. "We don't even go to church," Sue would remind her husband. For years, she had attempted to get her husband to attend church, but he always refused. His new habit was peculiar, to say the least.

Sting and his family finally made the move during the summer of 1998, and the reunion was complete. Sting and Jeff, along with their families, spent many hours together catching up. Earlier that year, Sting and Sue had made several trips to California to look for a new place to live. On one particular night, Jeff and Lori decided it was time to put things into a supernatural perspective. Lori went to their bedroom and quickly came back with a diary in hand. She started reading an entry from nearly a decade earlier that detailed a dream she had about Sting in which he had moved back. She also played a cassette recording from a service in November of 1992 in which a prophetic message was given to Jeff and Lori, indicating that the foundation for their family would be completed in five years. It was in November of 1997 that Sting had driven a posthole in his front yard in Atlanta and placed a "For Sale" sign there.

"When Lori read that diary entry, I was completely enthralled," Sting says. "I wanted to know every detail. It just fascinated me so much, and I needed to know more. I had been reading Hal

Lindsey books, and I was really curious about the book of Revelation and end-times, and it affected me."

He was only two months into his new Christian life when Sting realized he needed some time away from the ring to completely refocus his life. Following a loss to Bret Hart at *Halloween Havoc* on October 25, 1998, Sting took a three-month sabbatical from wrestling. Sting was nowhere to be found on either televised events or house shows. Sting used the time to strengthen a family that hadn't always been his first priority. He is convinced that his commitment to

"It was a real touchy situation. They all knew that I was different, and they all knew that I'd changed. For the most part, everybody accepted it. . . . They all knew that it was a good thing that had happened to me."

keeping God first has made all of the difference in his roles as a husband and father. "My wife and children are first now," he says. "They're first, and they're always going to be first. It took me a long time to get to that stage. I'm glad my life changed the way that it did."

When Sting returned to full-time action in January 1999, he was clearly a changed man. There was no hiding behind the face paint and the Sting persona. In fact, Sting was ready and willing to share his newfound faith with everyone in the locker room. Individually and in small groups, he told them all. Hogan, Flair, Luger, the Steiners, and Eric Bischoff were just a few who heard of his changed life from their longtime friend and colleague.

"It was a real touchy situation," Sting says. "They all knew that I was different, and they all knew that I'd changed. For the most part, everybody accepted it. They know me, and I think respected me for who I was and what my choices were and the integrity I displayed. They all knew that it was a good thing that had happened to me."

But just as soon as Sting was settling into the somewhat familiar surroundings, a new wrinkle was added to the multi-talented entertainer's life: acting. Sting had toyed with the idea of acting on the small screen as early as 1996, thanks to an opportunity Hulk Hogan had afforded him. While the two were flying between cities on a WCW tour of Japan, Hogan asked Sting to guest star in four episodes of the short-lived syndicated series "Thunder in Paradise." "That was when I decided this was something I wanted to do," he says.

Sting started taking classes to learn more about the craft. He knew there was much to learn about the differences between the over-the-top antics he describes as "playing to the balcony" and a less-is-more mentality. Sting's next break was in the independent film *The Real Reason (Men Commit Crimes)*. The movie aired on pay-per-view briefly and then went straight to video, but its arthouse appeal provided a boost for Sting's burgeoning career. His only other acting jobs up to that point were featured performances as Sting in commercials for Sprite and MasterCard's WCW signature series.

In 1999, Sting's acting career took a huge step forward, thanks to the TNT original film *Shutterspeed*, in which he co-starred with Daisy Fuentes. In the action/thriller, Sting portrays Riley Cooper, a narcotics cop who is drawn into a homicide investigation after his best friend is murdered. It was Sting's first opportunity to showcase his improving acting skills in a national release. Despite the brutal travel arrangements—Sting flew between Vancouver, Southern California, and various *Nitro* locations for six weeks—he managed to maintain his commitment to keeping Sue and the boys first. He received a little relief in early February 2000 when the TV movie finally aired, but only thanks to a pair of nagging injuries. Later that year, he would play himself as Sting in the feature film *Ready to Rumble*.

During that time, Sting became increasingly concerned with the direction his profession was heading. WCW's head writers were now the former WWF team of Vince Russo and Ed Ferrera. Russo had developed a reputation for pushing the moral limits and was largely responsible for the WWF's more adult-oriented themes. "We had our TV rating change from PG-TV to TV-14, the same rating that WWF has," Sting says. "Vince Russo and company pushed the envelope as far as they could every week. As long as they had that TV-14 rating, I believed they were going to keep pushing it until it got to be too much."

In two separate stints as head writer, Russo did as Sting predicted, yet the determined wrestler avoided involvement with the adult-oriented angles. As Sting, he continued to capture the imagination of his fans and remained a favorite at all WCW events. He was awarded a shot at the World Heavyweight title shot against Booker T strictly based on Internet voting, and was tabbed by WCW's female fans as their favorite. Two of the reasons they gave were his loyalty and his Christian beliefs. Sting found himself traveling to Australia, England, and Germany for hugely successful WCW tours.

But perhaps the most intriguing aspect of that year came in the form of an extended in-ring feud with perennial heel Vampiro. For several weeks, the two battled in a classic storyline of good versus evil, one that Sting hoped would end with the light overcoming the darkness. At times it seemed as if the battles were portrayed as a pseudo-spiritual melodrama. Other times, their dark nature seemed to border on sacrilege. Throughout the ordeal, Sting remained hopeful someone in the viewing audience would see a veiled retelling of the gospel.

One particular match found Sting and Vampiro fighting in a graveyard. The encounter came to a screeching halt when Vampiro struck Sting in the head with a tombstone, leaving him for dead in an open grave. Later, during the live television broadcast of *Nitro*, Vampiro gloated over his victory when suddenly

Sting emerged to triumphantly defeat his nemesis. All the while, the announcers were proclaiming that "Sting's alive" and "He's come back from the dead." Not until later did Sting realize that this had all occurred the day after Easter and how closely the tale resembled the story of Christ's death and resurrection.

Throughout winter and until spring of 2001, Sting took another leave of absence, this one due to an elbow injury in which several bone chips were removed. During his time off, he was able to focus on his two sons, Garrett and Steven, and spend a good deal of time helping Jeff at their home church. The break also allowed him to consider taking more speaking engagements and making personal ministry appearances. One such opportunity took the superstar to a nearby medium-confinement juvenile facility where he spoke to a group of troubled teens.

By February of 2001, Sting was preparing to get back into the ring. Eric Bischoff was working a deal with a company called Fusient to purchase WCW from Turner. Sting was excited about the possibilities. Bischoff had promised to clean up WCW and make it family friendly again. Nothing could have sounded better to Sting's ears. He was nearing a comeback as the unexpected news slowly leaked: Not only had Fusient's deal fallen through, but also it now looked as if Vince McMahon was going to purchase his competition. With many of WCW's staple wrestlers left out of the equation, Sting found himself pursuing his other dreams more actively. He now plans to further his career in television and film while leaving the door open for whatever wrestling opportunities may come his way. Long term, Sting desires to minister in some capacity at his home church, alongside brother and pastor Jeff.

"I see myself as being very active," Sting says. "I am a part of the body of that church. I've been so involved when I'm not on the road, and I'm looking forward to the day where I can be involved always."

Sting's time away from the ring opened his eyes to another possibility as well. He sees a great opportunity for him and Sue to minister together in some capacity. Just a few years after he almost lost his wife, the two are now closer than ever. "I love my wife very much," Sting says. "God is the most important thing in my life, then Sue is next. I can't describe how much our relationship means to me. I'm look forward to spending the rest of my life with her. It's been amazing to see how God has been working in her life."

Whether Sting's ministry takes him on the road for speaking engagements or simply plants him firmly at home, he has made a determination to never back down from the gospel message that saved his marriage, his family, and his life.

"People can talk about religion, and people can talk about God," he says. "They can talk about being spiritual, but when you mention Jesus Christ, people cringe. I'm glad I accepted Christ when I did. My life is better than it's ever been. I just want to help bring as many people as I can to Christ. That's the most important thing to me now."

STiNG

FULL NAME: Steven James Borden

NICKNAMES: Sting, Flash

BIRTHDATE: March 20, 1959

BIRTHPLACE: Omaha, Nebraska

HOMETOWN: Los Angeles, California

EDUCATION: William S. Hart High School, Newhall, California; College of the Canyons Junior College

HEIGHT: 6'3"

WEIGHT: 256 lbs.

FAMILY: Sue (wife); Steven, Garrett (sons); Gracie (daughter)

PRO WRESTLING DEBUT: 1985

PROMOTIONS: Mid-South, UWF, NWA, WCW

TITLES HELD: UWF World Tag Team (w/ Eddie Gilbert 2x, w/ Rick Steiner); NWA World Heavyweight; WCW International World Heavyweight (2x); NWA World Television; WCW World Tag Team (w/ Lex Luger, w/ The Giant, w/ Kevin Nash); WCW World Heavyweight (6x); WCW United States (2x); Jim Crockett Memorial Tag Team Tournament (w/ Lex Luger); King of Cable Tournament; European Cup

FINISHING MOVES: Scorpion Deathlock, Stinger Splash, Scorpion Deathdrop

FAVORITE FEUD: vs. Ric Flair

WORST INJURY: Injured left patella tendon in knee in 1990 at Clash of the Champions

TULLY BLANCHARD

CHAPTER 4

TULLY BLANCHARD

CHAPTER 4

t was 4:03 A.M. when it finally hit him. After three hours of anger, remorse, and self-pity, the words came out of nowhere.

"Jesus, take over my life," he said.

At that very moment, a peace came over Tully Blanchard like he'd never experienced before. It was a peace that soothed the painful shot he had just taken to his pride and to his pocketbook. Blanchard's successful runs through the National Wrestling Alliance (NWA) and World Wrestling Federation (WWF) resulted in big paychecks and a lofty lifestyle to match. His luxurious home in Charlotte, North Carolina, was accompanied by the token Mercedes-Benz parked in his garage. Blanchard was preparing for a triumphant return to World Championship Wrestling (formerly Mid-Atlantic Championship Wrestling) and a reformation of the legendary Four Horsemen. But instead, the results of a "confidential" failed drug test had leaked out to his new bosses, and his chance at a $750,000, three-year deal was history. It was supposed to be Blanchard's big score, his last hurrah in an industry to which he'd literally given blood and sweat. Tonight, it was time for the tears.

"Your life is going to be OK," Blanchard heard a comforting voice say.

It was November 13, 1991, and the changes Blanchard was about to experience would be a far cry from the life he had once lived. It was a life that revolved around professional wrestling and all of its excesses. It was a life he had never planned but certainly seemed destined to fulfill.

Blanchard grew up the son of pro wrestler and promoter Joe Blanchard. Born in Calgary, Ontario, he spent a mere two months in Canada before his family moved to Texas, where his father had bought into the Southwest Championship Wrestling promotion. Blanchard never found his roots permanently until fifth grade, when the family settled down in San Antonio. He can't remember when he actually started helping his father with the business. Blanchard just remembers it was one of life's constants.

By the time Blanchard entered Winston Churchill High School, football had become his new love. His athletic pedigree was apparent from the moment he stepped on the field. Blanchard was the team's starting quarterback for three seasons, and soon the college recruiters came calling. He ended up at Southern Methodist University, where Hayden Fry was the coach. Midway through his freshman season, Fry was fired, and Blanchard's hopes for the starting quarterback position effectively went down the drain. The new coaches moved him to fullback, then defensive end, where he made second team. He did see action on the kick-off squad, but it wasn't enough to keep him at SMU. Just before his sophomore season, Blanchard dropped out of school and went back home to work with the wrestling promotion.

Southwest Championship Wrestling was a staple throughout the state of Texas and the region. Blanchard helped produce the television shows for several months before finally deciding to get back to football. He transferred to West Texas State, but before he even took a snap, his long-term career was severely hindered by a serious car wreck. Fortunate that the crash did not take his life, Blanchard instead had to deal with severed muscles that left a scar from his right pectoral muscle, over his shoulder, and down the side of his back. Although he had spent three years as the starting quarterback, Blanchard's throwing ability was no longer NFL quality. While on that team, he met two other future wrestling stars: Tito Santana, who was Blanchard's tight end, and Ted DiBiase, who played defensive tackle. His college days had opened the door to a negative influence that would stay with him for more than a decade.

"I got into drugs and alcohol in college," Blanchard says. "That was the way you grew up in the '70s. Then when you get into wrestling, you have the money and free time. I didn't do anything while I was wrestling that I didn't already do in college."

Blanchard took his first shot at wrestling during the summer before his senior year. Both he and DiBiase took advantage of the new NCAA rule that allowed athletes to compete professionally in other sports without losing their amateur status. After spending the summer with Georgia Championship Wrestling, Blanchard came back and finished his last year. DiBiase did not, but instead pursued wrestling full-time. "I didn't really have any career goals in wrestling then," Blanchard says. "I was there to play football."

Once he graduated with a communications degree in 1977, that all changed. Knowing his NFL chances were slim to none, Blanchard moved to Florida to work the independent wrestling circuit. Later that year, he went to work for Jim Crockett's Mid-Atlantic Championship Wrestling promotion, part of the old NWA coalition. By the end of the year, he was ready to return to San Antonio and jump back into business with his father. Blanchard had accumulated several months of experience in front of and behind the camera. He had also studied radio and television at West Texas State and felt prepared to lead the business into the burgeoning cable television industry. Blanchard and his father bought an abandoned grocery store in San Antonio and taped their shows in a makeshift arena. The promotion also paid USA Network for a weekly television airing of its shows.

Unfortunately, Blanchard's alcohol and cocaine problems, along with his role as the consummate wrestling star, got in the way. "Most of the downfall can be attributed to me," Blanchard admits. "I didn't have a disciplined vision of where we were going. I was too busy being a star. Without vision, you perish."

Although Blanchard had left the business temporarily to get his life back in order, the damage was already done. Wrestlers were consistently overpaid, and the promotion had little left over to show for its efforts. Southwest Championship Wrestling ultimately lost its television package to Vince McMahon, who purchased the

rights on behalf of the WWF. By the time Blanchard was ready to return to wrestling, there was nothing left for him in San Antonio. Southwest Championship Wrestling had gone out of busi-

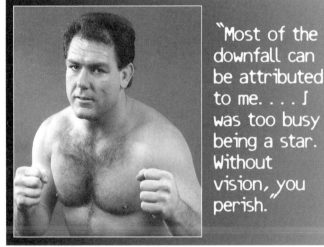

"Most of the downfall can be attributed to me. . . . I was too busy being a star. Without vision, you perish."

ness, and it was time for him to move on. In 1978, another family tragedy took place, this one much more painful than the loss of business. Blanchard's sixteen-year old brother was killed in a car accident and his parents were devastated. The death of their son ultimately led to their salvation, and they started attending church. Blanchard did not. He wouldn't darken the doors of any religious establishment for twelve more years.

Blanchard's next move was in early 1984, to Bob Geigel's Kansas

City-based Tri-States promotion. Affectionately referred to as "Siberia," Blanchard hated the cold weather and the equally cold and cavernous arenas that made Tri-States the most infamous promotion, at least from the wrestlers' perspective. Blanchard made the best of his one-month stay. He was perfecting his craft under the watchful eye of Johnny Valentine. Valentine would critique all of Blanchard's matches, then give him pointers on how to improve his performance. The hard work paid off during one particular shining moment in St. Louis. Jim Crockett was in attendance that night as Blanchard squared off against Buzz Tyler. "It was a showstopper," Blanchard says. "We really tore the house down that night."

Back at the hotel, he made sure to buddy up to Crockett and Dory Funk Jr. at the bar. The wrestling talk was limited but fruitful.

"Jimmy, you need to hire me," Blanchard boldly said. "I'll make you lots of money."

"Call me on Monday when we're not drinking, and I'll give you a start date," Crockett replied.

True to his word, Crockett brought Blanchard back to North Carolina to work for Mid-Atlantic Championship Wrestling. It was clearly a pivotal point in his career, just the break he needed. By the time Blanchard made his debut on February 14, 1984, he was a seasoned six-year veteran, so it didn't take long for him to get his first shot at the coveted title belt. Later that summer, he was already wearing the Mid-Atlantic Television Title belt (which later became the NWA World Television Title) and was involved in a still-famous angle with Ricky "The Steamboat" Dragon. According to the storyline, Blanchard was so confident he could take on any challenger that he put up $10,000 for anyone who could beat him in twenty minutes. Steamboat took the bait, and the two battled four times in matches that lasted from twenty to fifty minutes. The feud culminated at *Starrcade '84* when Blanchard disposed of his foe in fifteen minutes. His sharply dressed image, along with his flamboyant interview style, was now a staple within the NWA. With

"Back in those days, you created your own character. You were either good at it or you weren't."

manager J.J. Dillon and a sassy, blonde-haired valet named Baby Doll by his side, Blanchard had the makings of a true wrestling superstar.

"Back in those days, you created your own character," Blanchard says. "You were either good at it or you weren't. The Steamboat matches really put me over the top. That was a real boost to my career."

At the same time, Ric Flair was reemerging after a year on the road. Arn Anderson and Ole Anderson were also making names for themselves. By late 1985, the four found themselves developing a chemistry that ran deeper than just in-ring techniques and on-camera interviews. They all wore blazers with dress pants and dress shoes. If they weren't wearing ties around their necks, they were sporting gold chains. Cufflinks and sunglasses were their accessories of choice. It became a regular occurrence to see them bailing each other out.

"It just happened," Blanchard says. "It was a quirk of nature. It wasn't just somebody saying, 'We want to have four horsemen!' Ric and I dressed the part before then, and Arn just kind of did his thing. The fans took hold of it, and it exploded. It really was a phenomenon. The fans caught on, and then the promoters caught on. That's why is was so successful, because it wasn't promoter generated."

The progression of intertwining storylines ultimately brought the four men together, and in a TV interview, Arn Anderson made reference to the biblical Four Horsemen and the havoc they were to wreak, described in Revelation 6. The name was actually derived from a nickname given to the legendary Notre Dame defensive line. Four fingers raised to the sky suddenly meant instant excitement from the crowd. Groups of college kids started to show up on the front row dressed like the Four Horsemen, waving signs.

"We talked about our gimmicks," Blanchard says. "We very seldom talked about our opponents. We talked about being the best and being world champions. Then we went out and delivered the product. It was more of a doctrine on life, and people bought into it. It took me years to figure it out myself. It was certainly something that the wrestling business had never seen before, and it hasn't been the same since. They've tried to bring back the Four Horsemen, but it never worked because they never knew why it worked before. You can't duplicate something if you don't know why it worked."

"When you watched me wrestle, you got your money's worth. All of my matches were intense. That's why I was successful."

It was equally difficult to duplicate Blanchard's work ethic in the ring. His matches were rarely shorter than thirty minutes and often lasted longer than an hour. Blanchard bladed (cut himself) during almost every match, and his high threshold for self-inflicted pain made many an onlooker squeamish.

One of the best examples of Blanchard's insane ring antics took place at *Starrcade '85* in a cage match against the popular star Magnum T.A. The match took place in Greensboro, North Carolina, in front of 16,000 fans and was simulcast via closed circuit television to a crowd of 18,000 more fans in Atlanta's Omni Arena. Not only was the match for Blanchard's NWA U.S. Heavyweight belt, it was also an "I Quit" match. The match could not end until one of the opponents literally said those two words. After they had tossed each other into the cage and beat each other in the head with the microphone, leaving them both bleeding profusely, Blanchard's valet, Baby Doll, tossed a wooden chair into the ring. Instead of using the object in the traditional manner (that is, crashing it over the opponent's head or back), Blanchard broke the chair and pulled off a piece of a leg in such a way that it formed a crude stake. With Magnum T.A. on his back, Blanchard proceeded to aim the stake at his opponent's eye. Never able to connect, Blanchard lost the match when T.A. took the same stake to his brow and Blanchard uttered the magic words.

"When you watched me wrestle, you got your money's worth," Blanchard boasts. "All of my matches were intense. That's why I was successful. The way we wrestled, it looked a lot more believable. When I broke the chair and used it in the match, that just happened. It wasn't planned. Let's just say I'm very good at what I do."

In April of 1988, Blanchard's contract with Jimmy Crockett expired. There were no negotiations planned for him or his partner Arn Anderson. In the meantime, Crockett was in the process of selling his promotions to Turner Broadcasting System (TBS). Several wrestlers were asked to attend meetings with the prospective new owners. Blanchard assessed the situation in a way that offended Crockett and Dusty Rhodes, the company's biggest star, who was also booking or planning most of the matches. As punishment, Blanchard was left off the travel roster for the next set of shows. "They took me off the plane, and I had to drive to the arenas," Blanchard says. "I didn't feel like I needed to be spanked, so I decided it was time to go."

Before he could leave the promotion, he had one last task to perform. He and Anderson were the Tag Team champions, which meant they were required to drop the belts by losing a match to the Midnight Express in Philadelphia. Anderson was not on bad terms with Crockett, but to Blanchard's surprise, he also made the move. It was off to New York and the WWF, where Vince McMahon Jr. gladly welcomed two of his competition's key players. Blanchard was sure this huge step would take his career to new heights. Instead, the proverbial grass on the other side was no different a shade of green.

"Even though we became the WWF Tag Team champions, we hoped that Vince had hired us to improve his company," Blanchard says. "Time told, that wasn't the case. He had hired us to hurt the other company. That was disappointing. We were main eventers, but we didn't end up making any more money than we did before. It ended up being a lateral move. It was a very good move by Vince. When we left [NWA], it destroyed the Four Horsemen and killed the company for a number of years. It would have been another thing if he had hired us to expand his company and expand our careers, but our careers were insignificant to him. We were just pawns."

That's not to say that Blanchard didn't have his highlights with the WWF. He and Anderson (now known as the Brainbusters) worked memorable programs with some of the best tag teams around. Their matches against the Rockers, featuring Marty Jannetty and rising star Shawn Michaels, were especially explosive. Blanchard also had the opportunity to wrestle under the lights of Madison Square Garden in New York, a venue he describes as "the epitome of entertainment and sports." But the good times in the ring were nothing compared to the wild happenings backstage and in the hotels after the shows. Blanchard had found his way back into the drug culture and was once again using cocaine. According to Blanchard, most of the wrestlers were using drugs of some sort, marijuana being the most popular stimulant. Yet somehow, it was *his* drug habit that stirred up the most controversy.

"I'd cut a deal with WCW for $750,000 over three years," Blanchard explains. "I gave notice to Vince, but he wasn't going to release us from our contracts until after *Survivor Series*, which was two and a half months away. In the process, I failed a drug test before a Saturday afternoon show at the Philadelphia Spectrum. They suspended me on October 2, then Flair called me on November 13 about one o'clock in the morning to tell me that WCW was going to renege on their deal. Vince didn't want me going back to the other company, so he either told somebody or called them himself."

Blanchard may never know what really happened, but at this point, it doesn't seem to matter. He had hoped to retire from wrestling at age forty, and that quarter of a million dollars a year was the key. Even before the devastating news, Blanchard felt a strong need to make serious changes in his life. He just didn't know how to do it. The power of prayer combined with a personal setback turned out to be the most potent formula.

"My parents and people from their church had been praying for me for twelve years," Blanchard recalls. "God answers prayers. The Lord just took all that stuff away from me—drugs, alcohol, cussing. I was just changed. I talked to my dad a few days later on the phone, and he said I sounded different. I wasn't cussing. Before that night, the only time I'd used Christ's name was when I was cussing. Suddenly, I wasn't using those words anymore."

It took Blanchard a few weeks to feel comfortable enough to attend church. When he finally did, he found Central Church of God in Charlotte. It soon became his home church, where he eventually landed a full-time job on the ministry staff until moving to the hills of Rutherfordton, North Carolina, in 2000. Blanchard spent time as the church's activities director and men's minister, and eventually headed a prison evangelism ministry that he personally instituted. "I learned rapidly," Blanchard says. "When you have a great desire, the learning curve is high."

Blanchard's involvement with prison ministry came from the prompting of Jack Murphy (a.k.a. Murph the Surf), who told him about Bill Glass Prison Ministries in March of 1994. Doors opened for him to learn more about the ministry, and soon he was visiting prisons throughout North Carolina. He has recently expanded his ministry to include visits to all parts of the U.S. He now serves as a regional director for Bill Glass and is building a transitional worship center for recently released inmates. The facility will help train the men in both functional and spiritual matters in order to make them productive in society and in the church. Blanchard also founded the Exodus Foundation as a result of his calling into the prisons. It's a place to which he continually feels drawn.

"I take the message that it doesn't matter how bad you've messed up. If you allow Christ to fix it, He will."

TULLY BLANCHARD

"There's a lot of commonality when you've got the drug experience and that background," Blanchard says. "Jesus took hope to the hopeless. That's what we do. There's a high level of hopelessness in those prisons."

Blanchard has seen hundreds of men experience life-changing encounters with God. "It's a humbling thing to share the gospel

with anyone and know that God has called you to do it,"
Blanchard says. "I take the message that it doesn't matter how bad
you've messed up. If you allow Christ to fix it, He will."

TULLY BLANCHARD

FULL NAME: Tully Arthur Blanchard

BIRTHDATE: January 22, 1954

BIRTHPLACE: Calgary, Ontario

HOMETOWN: Rutherfordton, North Carolina

EDUCATION: Winston Churchill High School, San Antonio, Texas; West Texas State

HEIGHT: 5'11"

WEIGHT: 225

PROMOTIONS: Southwest Championship; FCW; NWA; Mid-Atlantic Championship; WCW; ECW; Georgia Championship

TITLES HELD: NWA Tag Team (w/ Arn Anderson); WWF Tag Team (w/ Arn Anderson); NWA World Television Title; Mid-Atlantic Television Title; NWA U.S. Heavyweight

FINISHING MOVE: Slingshot Suplex

FAVORITE FEUDS: Singles vs. Dusty Rhodes; Tag Team w/ Arn Anderson vs. the Rockers (Marty Jannetty and Shawn Michaels)

WORST INJURY: Separated shoulder; hyper-extended knee; broken ankle (three times)

NIKITA KOLOFF

CHAPTER 5

NIKITA KOLOFF
CHAPTER 5

The Charlotte air is thick with apprehension. Inside the sold-out arena, speculation runs wild among the thousands of fans in attendance. Their hero, "The American Dream"—Dusty Rhodes—deliberately and confidently strolls the aisle toward the ring. His blaring entrance music is usually met with deafening cheers. Tonight, there is silence.

Doesn't he see who's behind him? people in the crowd wonder. *Is his life in danger?*

It's a legitimate question. The evil Russian heel, Nikita Koloff, is lurking a mere ten feet behind Rhodes. His menacing presence is captivating, complete with shaved head, goatee, and expression-less face. Was he the mystery partner that had been so heavily advertised, or merely a decoy waiting for his chance to attack? Nothing happens, yet the tension grows. Rhodes steps through the door of the cage that surrounds the ring. Ole Anderson and J.J. Dillon of the Four Horsemen meet him inside. The two immediately begin to beat Rhodes down to the mat. Koloff looks on from outside.

"Somebody help Dusty!" the fans scream.

Koloff walks to the barricade and pauses. He takes time to scan the entire building. He steps up to the cage door and once again stops to look around. Rhodes continues to take a severe beating from his opponents. Koloff enters the cage and deliberately inches towards the ropes. He pauses again. Anderson spots Koloff. He breaks away from his thrashing of Rhodes and casually moves toward the Russian Nightmare. Anderson is met with a brutal array of punches, and Koloff quickly deposits his beaten body through the cage door. As soon as the first blow lands, the crowd roars in unison, seeming to lift the roof off the building. Together, Rhodes and Koloff finish off Dillon to end the match.

Chants of "Nikita! Nikita! Nikita!" echo throughout the arena for a solid fifteen minutes. The same male wrestling fans that had once literally spit on Koloff are now ripping off their shirts to mimic his muscular posing and are sticking their tongues out for good measure. Koloff and Rhodes, once mortal enemies, are now called "The Superpowers." On that fateful night in 1986, Koloff instantly went from the most hated wrestler to one of the industry's most beloved superstars. It was a major turn and undoubtedly one of professional wrestling's best-kept secrets.

But it wouldn't be Koloff's last turn or even his most important. That would come six years later. In fact, Koloff's life had already been full of turns and the unpredictable twists that often accompany them. Koloff, born Nelson Scott Simpson in Minneapolis,

Minnesota, was the youngest of four children born to Pete and Olive Simpson. Koloff's mother was born in England near the Scottish border; his father was French Canadian with an Eastern European heritage. The two met during World War I. Pete Simpson left the family when Koloff was just two years old. The next several years would bring constant financial struggle for the single-parent household.

"My mother did the best she could," Koloff says. "She had a very good work ethic, but she didn't make very much money. We were a welfare family, and we lived in the ghettos of Minneapolis. I can remember the days in elementary school when I would get special food tickets and the embarrassment of it. That made an impression on me more than anything."

On that fateful night in 1986, Koloff instantly went from the most hated wrestler to one of the industry's most beloved superstars.

Koloff took matters into his own hands. By the sixth grade, he had taken on a paper route and began saving money. When he started playing football in the ninth grade, he hired a younger boy to take his route for him. Koloff would collect the money, then pay his "employee" a percentage. He also spent time working at fast food establishments and as a busboy at a fancy hotel restaurant.

"I worked for everything I have," Koloff says. "Nothing was hand-ed to me. It gave me a greater appreciation for earning things. I was entrepreneurial at an early age. Reflecting back, I can certain-ly say that my mother's work ethic had an effect on me. Just see-ing her provide for us was instrumental in my success."

When Koloff was twelve years old, he first caught a glimpse of what health and fitness could do for him. He started reading *Iron Man* magazine and was instantly hooked on the idea of looking like the "big muscle heads" that were featured throughout its pages. "I bought a little 110-pound weight set with my paper route money," Koloff recalls. "It was a plastic set that I kept in the garage, and I started working out."

Koloff also met Gerry McFarland, a health teacher and gymnas-tics coach at the junior high school. He was a competitive body-builder and became an instant role model for Koloff, who would spend most of his spare time at school in McFarland's classroom. The room was loaded with weightlifting equipment, most of which McFarland himself had designed. Koloff would continue to train under the teacher's direction throughout high school and much of his college years. The training helped Koloff develop as a foot-ball player. He had started playing football in seventh grade, and by the time he reached high school, he was making a big impact. During his junior and senior years, he was a two-way starter at the tight end and defensive end positions.

NIKITA KOLOFF

Koloff's success led him straight to Golden Valley Lutheran College, a small junior college with a long history of great athletics. By this time, his father was back in the picture. Pete had become a Christian and was trying to mend some of his past relationships. Simpson would attend many of his son's games, and they would often go out to eat afterwards. "I never grew up with a dad, so he was more like a friend," Koloff explains. "I've never harbored bitterness or anger towards him. I just wasn't drawn to him."

Midway through his freshman season, Koloff's team was on the road facing Thief River Falls Junior College. His season was going as planned. Koloff was the starting tight end. He was averaging close to twenty-five yards per catch and had scored several touchdowns. Now he was running a bomb route, while the split end was running a down-and-across pattern. The referee's whistle blew the play dead, and the players all eased up. One of Thief River Falls' defensive backs shoved Koloff's teammate in the back and sent him flying. Out of the corner of his eye, Koloff could see something coming his way. Before he could react, his teammate was cross body-blocked below Koloff's right knee. The snapping sound was loud and clear; Koloff's tibia and fibula had been broken.

"I was on the field for over an hour," Koloff remembers. "The trainer and the coaches didn't know what to do. We were six hours from the Twin Cities, and there was no ambulance at the stadium. The trainer made the mistake of cutting the tape off my ankles. When he did that, my ankle just ballooned eight times its normal size, and they couldn't get an air cast on it. Nothing would fit. I was an eighteen-year old punk kid who was just in shock. I can remember lying on the field. I wouldn't open my eyes. I was doing the 'why me?' thing. My life was over. My football career was over. No NFL. It's over."

Koloff spent the next seventeen days in the hospital and six weeks in a cast. His doom-and-gloom attitude improved considerably after a chance meeting with an old high school coach. The two hadn't always been always on the best of terms, so when the coach told his former player that no one had ever come back from such an injury, that was all the motivation Koloff needed. The following summer, he trained with a steel plate and screws on his tibia. The first hit he took during fall camp sent him to the ground writhing with pain. There was no break, but he decided to sit out the rest of the season nonetheless.

After returning in healthy condition, Koloff was ready to move on. He and teammate Joe Laurenaitis ended up at Moorhead State, a small four-year college in Minnesota. Laurenaitis would later became a wrestling superstar under the name "Animal" with the famous "Road Warriors" or "Legion of Doom" tag team.

Moorhead State was a National Association of Intercollegiate Athletics (NAIA) powerhouse, and by Koloff's senior season, the team was contending for a national championship. As the regular season was nearing its end and the playoffs were right around the corner, Koloff once again saw his fortunes take a turn for the worse. With just two minutes left in the first half, Moorhead State was winning 52-6. Koloff was playing left tight end on a flood play. All of the receivers and backs flooded to the left, allowing Koloff to delay block for the pass, then slip back across the field to the right. He was wide open and caught the ball. The sun was shining brightly under a clear autumn sky. Koloff saw nothing but real estate and the goal line in front of him. With a linebacker in hot pursuit, Koloff turned up field, hoping to avoid the tackle. Instead, the defender caught him by the shoulder pad. His left foot, holding his entire weight, was firmly planted in the natural turf. The leg could do nothing but twist and snap. The play had taken place along his team's sideline, allowing Koloff to instinctively roll out of bounds. Like the infamous injury to Hall of Fame quarterback Joe Theismann of the Washington Redskins, Koloff's bone had broken through the skin, much to his teammates' horror.

"I'd been through this before and I was more mature, so I was telling the trainer what to do," Koloff says. "That injury did get caught on film, and several of the guys told me later that when they watched it, they got sick. It really freaked out a lot of the freshmen."

Koloff was once again sent into rehabilitation. He graduated from Moorhead State and moved back home, living on his own in Minneapolis. Koloff became a self-described gym rat, spending eight hours a day working out and using the nights to earn money as a bouncer. He still hoped to fulfill his long-standing NFL dream. One night at the club where he worked, Koloff was involved with a scuffle and inexplicably re-injured his left leg. It was a hairline fracture through one of the screw holes that had held the metal plate in place. This time, the doctors decided to insert a permanent steel rod in his leg to insure against future breaks. A week later, he was back in the gym lifting weights and remained determined to play professional football.

Koloff spent much of 1983 training for a shot at the NFL. His friend Laurenaitis had since moved to Atlanta, where he was working for Georgia Championship Wrestling. On New Year's Day 1984, Koloff moved south to rehab in the company of his friend. He also had a tryout lined up with the Tampa Bay Bandits of the upstart United States Football League (USFL). Laurenaitis suggested that Koloff consider professional wrestling as a career. Koloff disagreed. "I didn't like wrestling as a kid," he admits. "I hated it."

Koloff returned to Minneapolis two months later to finish his training. Early that summer, Laurenaitis called his friend to tell him of an opportunity with promoter Jim Crockett. This was followed up by a call from Crockett himself. Koloff suddenly found himself intrigued by the possibility. "Be in my office June 4 with your head shaved bald," Crockett ordered.

Koloff did as he was told and arrived on the appointed day. He walked in Crockett's office in peak form. Koloff weighed 285 pounds, with just 8 percent body fat and a 34-inch waist. Crockett could hardly believe his eyes. He looked once, then did a double take. After having Koloff take off his shirt for a closer inspection, Crockett left the room and came back quickly with two other men.

"This is Ivan Koloff and Don Kernoble," Crockett said. "Guys, meet your new partner."

Later that day, the former Scott Simpson was given the nickname "Nikita Koloff" and took part in several television promotional spots. He was instructed to simply stand behind Koloff and Kernoble with his shirt off. The elder Koloff would introduce the newcomer as his nephew from Russia who was straight off the boat and spoke no English. *Shave my head and look mean*, Koloff thought. *This business is a piece of cake.*

The very next night, Koloff saw his first action in the ring. Before the ringing of the bell could fade, Koloff had pounded his adversary into submission. That was how things would be for several months to come. Opponents were told not to knock Koloff off his feet or they would be fired. His matches only lasted one or two minutes, sometimes less. Koloff would enter the ring, demolish his opponent for the victory, then beat them down even more for good measure—nothing technical. As time passed, Ivan Koloff would teach him more moves, and his time in the ring slowly increased. But what made Koloff a successful heel was the same work ethic that he'd carried since his youth.

"Just like everything I've done, I took it to the hilt," Koloff says. "I studied the Russian language. I learned to sign my name in Russian. I decided I wouldn't speak English anywhere outside of the car I was in. I didn't sign autographs. I didn't talk to anybody for months, and even when I started talking on TV, I still didn't talk outside the arena to fans. If they wanted an autograph, I just looked at them with a scowl."

Koloff's biggest step was to legally change his name from Scott Simpson to Nikita Koloff. While many thought that to be an extreme move, he believes it was the only sensible thing to do. He felt it was necessary to help solidify the character and cause people to truly buy into the Russian act. "I have people who tell me they really thought I was from Russia," Koloff proudly claims. "They were supposed to think that. It was my job."

Many wrestling historians have noticed a similarity between Koloff's quick rise to stardom and a more recent example. Is it coincidence that "The Russian Nightmare" can be so closely linked to current wrestling superstar Bill Goldberg? Koloff thinks not. "There's nothing new under the sun, and everything's been remanufactured," Koloff contends. "Terry Taylor developed [Goldberg's] character, and if you were to ask him, he would tell you that he patterned [Goldberg's] character after my character, my mannerisms, the whole nine yards. It might be just a duplication of my character, but that's the sincerest form of flattery."

In just two years, Koloff had become the biggest heel in wrestling. He was voted Most Hated Heel that year and achieved greatness along with Ivan Koloff and new partner Krusher Kruschev. The timing was perfect for Koloff's switch to the other side. After an epic seven-match feud with Terry Allen (a.k.a. Magnum T.A.), Koloff toured Japan. Upon returning, he learned of

Allen's career-ending car accident. His departure from wrestling left a void for Dusty Rhodes, who had tagged with Allen in a feud against the Four Horsemen. Rhodes needed a new partner, and being one of the company's top stars, he could choose anyone he wanted. Rhodes wanted Koloff, thus setting the stage for the emergence of "The Superpowers." The move lifted Koloff to a higher level of fame, but it didn't come without a price.

"In my rise to stardom, it certainly didn't sit well with a lot of the guys," Koloff admits. "Even the start of my career, because many guys had been there for seven, eight years trying to get a break. Then here comes this guy who's never even hit a ring rope. My babyface turn didn't sit well with many of the guys, either."

In just two years, Koloff had become the biggest heel in wrestling. He was voted Most Hated Heel that year . . . the timing was perfect for Koloff's switch to the other side.

For the next two years, Koloff and Rhodes headlined many shows across the country and abroad. "The American Dream" and "The Russian Nightmare" became the unlikeliest pair of heroes. But outside the ring, Koloff was facing a personal nightmare. His fiancée, Mandy, was battling Hodgkin's disease, and he requested some time off to help her deal with the sickness. The two eventually married and took a trip to Greece, where Mandy received special medical treatment. Koloff then took his wife back to her hometown of Huntsville, Alabama, where she spent the last six weeks of her life in an intensive care unit. During that time, Ric Flair was booking the matches for WCW and consistently asked Koloff to come back. Until now, few people have heard of one particular meeting Koloff had at Flair's house where "The Nature Boy" offered him the World Heavyweight Title in exchange for an immediate return. Koloff respectfully declined. When Mandy passed away, Koloff returned to North Carolina but didn't have the desire or emotional strength for the rigorous wrestling lifestyle.

"They called me up a week after Mandy died and asked me if I would come back," Koloff says. "I told them again that I appreciated the offer, but I wasn't ready yet. It took me about six months before I got back into the ring again."

When Koloff did finally return, Ted Turner now owned WCW, and many changes had taken place behind the scenes. Prior to his first leave of absence, charter pilots were told to never leave the runway without Ric Flair, Dusty Rhodes, Magnum T.A., or Nikita Koloff. If anyone else arrived late, the plane would leave as scheduled. Now, the athletes were required to travel to Atlanta and fly out from there. Several wrestlers remained in Charlotte and had to make the four-hour drive just to catch the company flight. Koloff's entrepreneurial spirit gave him a better idea.

"I tried and tried to convince the company that the airline tickets were actually cheaper flying out of Charlotte," Koloff says. "But they never listened to me. That was back in the days of refundable tickets. I took the tickets they gave me, and I became my own travel agent. I'd trade my ticket in for a flight out of Charlotte and get a refund on the difference. I literally made two or three thousand dollars doing that."

Despite his professional frustrations, Koloff was recovering from the tragic loss of Mandy. He had found himself drawing close to her best friend, Victoria, who had two young daughters, Teryn and Tawni, from a previous marriage. Eventually, with the prodding of Laurenaitis, Koloff mustered up the courage to ask Victoria for a date. In 1990, less than a year later, the two were married. The Koloffs have since added Kendra and Kolby to the family.

For the next two years, Koloff constantly fought battles with the WCW regarding the direction of his character. The bookers tried to turn him back to a heel, but he refused. His pairing with Lex Luger ultimately failed, so his next stop was a run with the equally popular Sting. The union seemed to work out better, but contract disputes put Koloff back on the shelf for another six months. Upon returning, he picked up where he left off and entered into a feud with Big Van Vader. Known for his brutally stiff wrestling style, the enormous Vader was quite a challenge even for Koloff. On November 7, 1992, the two faced each other in what seemed to be a routine battle, which instead ended up being Koloff's last match.

"We were fighting on the floor, and [Vader] took a charge at me and clotheslined me in the back of the head," Koloff describes. "My left arm went numb. It was that sensation of sleeping on your arm, then you wake up and you can't move it. For the next several minutes of the match, my arm was just dangling. Finally, the feeling started to come back, and I was able to finish the match. I was planning to get my neck checked out the next day as a precaution. About five o'clock in the morning, I woke up and felt this pain all the way down to my lower abdomen. It turned out that I had a hernia from picking up Vader, and I had a jammed vertebra that resulted in a pinched nerve in my neck. The doctors never told me I couldn't go back to wrestling but that it would be in my best interest to quit."

By that time, Koloff and Victoria's first child together, Kendra, was nearly six months old. The intense travel was wearing Koloff down, and he longed to be at home where he could help raise the family. He was also tired of the games WCW was playing in the ring, so he simply walked away. There was no fanfare, no pleas to return, not even so much as one phone call asking if he was OK. "They didn't really care," Koloff says.

At the same time, Koloff had begun a season of soul-searching. He and Victoria knew that they wanted to rear their family with positive moral values and realized that the Christian faith would be the best avenue. Koloff didn't have much baggage from his wrestling days. He was never involved with the drug culture and always returned to his hotel room while the others stayed out late drinking. Still, living a good, moral life wasn't enough to fill the void that engulfed Koloff's heart.

"I had all the stuff," Koloff says. "I'd traveled all over the world. I'd experienced the different cultures. I had the cars, the big house, and the family. I had fame and fortune. But there was something missing. I knew there had to be something more to life."

After spending a year at a Lutheran church, the family eventually settled down at First Assembly of God in Concord, North Carolina. On one particular Sunday morning in October of 1993,

"I had all the stuff. I'd traveled all over the world. . . . I had the cars, the big house, and the family. I had fame and fortune. But there was something missing. I knew there had to be something more to life."

Koloff was about to make a life-changing decision. Victoria knew something was going on with her husband when she saw him put a $100 bill in the offering plate. At the conclusion of the pastor's message that morning, he asked the million-dollar question: "Who has not accepted Jesus Christ as their personal Savior?" Koloff didn't care what his wife thought or even what his wrestling buddies were going to think. He made up his mind quickly and walked the aisle down to the altar. After the service, an older gentleman introduced himself to Nikita as "Buddy."

"In 1988, I saw you on TV," a tearful Buddy told Nikita. "The Holy Spirit spoke to my heart and told me, 'Start praying for that man's salvation.' For five years I've prayed for you. I wasn't even going to come to church today. I've been ill most of the week. But for some reason, the Spirit kept telling me to go to church. Of all the churches in the world, I was able to sit back in this church and watch you pray at that altar."

Buddy died just a few weeks after that encounter. And while the old man's life was ending, Koloff's real life was just beginning. In March of 1995, he first heard Terrance Rose preach in a revival

"A lot of people think that when you get saved, it's the end. But it's really only the beginning. There's so much to learn and so much to do for Christ."

service on a Friday night. Koloff spent the next twenty-two weeks working with Rose's "Campaign for Christ" ministry while traveling across the southeastern U.S. Rose, a former British soccer player turned successful businessman in South Africa, has been a spiritual mentor to Koloff, who has since created his own "Koloff for Christ" ministry. He has traveled to such places as Singapore, Angola, Moldova, Colombia, Trinidad, and South Africa. Koloff has helped build churches and schools, and has also been part of large evangelistic crusades.

NIKITA KOLOFF

Koloff calls his marriage a "tag team in ministry." He and Victoria also run a successful pre-paid legal service. Both find themselves on the road often, either in business or ministry. According to Koloff, God has helped them find balance in their home while maintaining a slew of business clients and speaking engagements. He has seen lives changed in developing countries and in his own backyard. Koloff's testimony has made an impact on a wide range of people that include some of his closest friends in the wrestling business. It's a testimony he intends to share for many years to come.

"This has been a phenomenal experience," Koloff says. "God has orchestrated all of this. A lot of people think that when you get saved, it's the end. But it's really only the beginning. There's so much to learn and so much to do for Christ."

NikiTA KOLOFF

FULL NAME: Nikita S. Koloff (legally changed from Nelson Scott Simpson)

NICKNAMES: The Russian Nightmare

BIRTHDATE: March 9, 1959

BIRTHPLACE: Minneapolis, Minnesota

HOMETOWN: Mount Pleasant, North Carolina

EDUCATION: Robinsdale High School, Robinsdale, Minnesota; Golden Valley Junior College; Moorhead State

HEIGHT: 6'2"

WEIGHT: 275 lbs.

FAMILY: Victoria (wife); Teryn, Tawni, Kendra, and Kolby (daughters)

PRO WRESTLING DEBUT: June 5, 1984

FIRST MATCH: Defeated Brett Hart (Barry Horowitz)

PROMOTIONS: NWA, AWA, WCW

TITLES HELD: NWA National Heavyweight, NWA U.S. Heavyweight, NWA World Television, NWA World Tag Team (w/ Ivan Koloff 2x), NWA World Six Man Tag (w/ Ivan Koloff and Krusher Krushchev); NWA/UWF World Television Unification

FINISHING MOVE: Russian Sickle (running clothesline)

FAVORITE FEUDS: Singles vs. Magnum T.A. (World Series of Wrestling), vs. Ric Flair; Tag Team (w/ Ivan Koloff) vs. The Road Warriors

WORST INJURY: Lower back injury vs. Flair; Neck injury and hernia vs. Big Van Vader

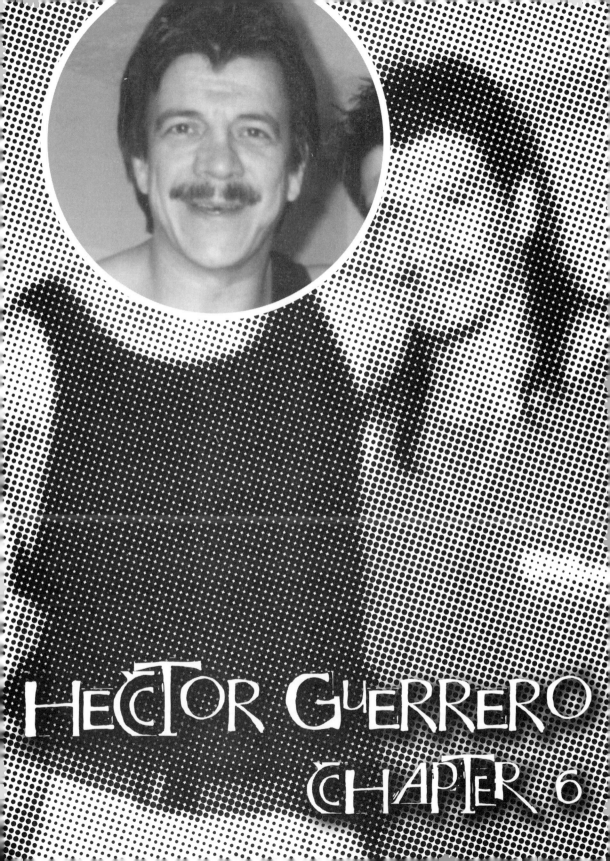

HECTOR GUERRERO

CHAPTER 6

HECTOR GUERRERO
CHAPTER 6

Hector Guerrero makes sure he gets it right. He watches his words carefully and corrects any questionable comments as quickly as they leave his mouth. Guerrero has spent the majority of his adult life making up for mistakes that he made in his young adult years. Now determined to "walk the walk" and not just "talk the talk," the Mexican-American wrestling star considers the words he speaks to be a key component of a successful life.

"Anything that happens in my life, God should be given the glory," Guerrero says. "God has orchestrated everything in my life. I'm not talking about the bad. Those were my wrong doings. I don't blame anyone but myself. In fact, I thank God it didn't get any worse than it did."

Guerrero's path wasn't always so treacherous. His upbringing in a legendary wrestling family may not have provided the most normal lifestyle, but it was stable and solidly based on his parents' faith in Christ. Guerrero's story, like that of all second-generation wrestlers, is very much rooted in his genealogy. His father, Gory

Guerrero, was born in 1921 and was orphaned as a teenager. He became responsible for his sisters in Mexico. At a young age, Gory began wrestling with an organization based in Guadalajara. He quickly gained popularity among the local wrestling fans. In Guadalajara Gory met the original Mexican wrestling star, El Santo. From there, he moved to Mexico City and found himself rising to stardom as one of the most hated heels in the business. Gory claimed Mexican national welterweight and middleweight titles and a number of Mexican NWA titles as well. He is widely recognized as the inventor of the camel clutch hold and was also famous for a surfboard hold that was affectionately known as the "Gory Special."

"God blessed him," Guerrero says. "The Lord blessed him, and he was anointed. He became what they call in Mexico a legend. I don't believe we should say that. I believe we should say that the grace of God and the power of the Holy Spirit was a strong influence on my dad, and he became who he became, which was an outstanding star."

After establishing himself in the wrestling business, Gory met his wife through her brother, Enrique Yañez, also a Mexican wrestling star at the time. The two started a family shortly thereafter. A daughter, Cookie, and two sons, Chavo and Mando, came first; Chavo and Mando would go on to become wrestling stars in Mexico and in the U.S. as well. On October 1, 1954, Hector became the third of four sons, followed by younger sister Linda and younger brother Eddy. Eddy currently wrestles with the WWF after spending productive years with WCW, ECW, and various promotions in Mexico and Japan. All of the children were born in Mexico City with the exception of Eddy, who was born in El Paso, Texas, after the family moved to the U.S. One constant for the Guerrero family was their faithful church attendance at Trinity Baptist Church in El Paso.

"He was very strict about church every Sunday," Guerrero says about his father. "I gave my life to Jesus as a Baptist, but later on I pulled away because I never liked religion."

"Anything that happens in my life, God should be given the glory. . . . I'm not talking about the bad. Those were my wrong doings. I don't blame anyone but myself. In fact, I thank God it didn't get any worse than it did."

While Guerrero was still in junior high school, he had an encounter with God that he failed to understand and fully appreciate until several years later. His grandmother had come to stay with the family for an extended period of time. Guerrero and his brother shared a bunk bed, and a third bed in their room played host to the visiting matriarch. One night, Guerrero knelt at his bedside for nightly prayer. He felt a warm sensation enter his body that traveled from the top of his head all the way through the tips of his toes. It was a feeling that he would experience later as an adult with even greater intensity.

Guerrero tells of other supernatural accounts that took place later in his teenage years. He remembers having several dreams and one particular vision in which he saw the eyes of God. Guerrero vividly recalls seeing images in which he was sitting on the lap of God. He couldn't see His face, because He was looking down at an open book that was labeled "The Book of Life."

"He started opening the pages for me," Guerrero says. "The first page was a picture of stars. It was like a 3-D picture, and I could see into it. He opened the next page, and it was vegetation and animals and all of these beautiful things He was showing me. He closed the book, and I could see that it had markers. I saw one marker that said 'G,' and I realized it was 'G' for 'God.' When I opened that page, I was completely engulfed by light, and in my dream, I could see two eyes looking at me. I woke up from my dream, and I couldn't move a muscle. I tried to move and I wanted to move, but I just couldn't move. I felt a warm, oily feeling all over my body, and I didn't have a care in the world, and I could feel His love."

By the time Guerrero was in high school, Chavo and Mando were already following in their father's wrestling footsteps. But the younger Guerrero wasn't convinced that wrestling was for him. He was more interested in music than sports and at one point attempted to quit high school wrestling, much to his family's dismay.

"I was kind of pressured into it," Guerrero says. "I wanted to pursue a music career. I played trumpet, and I had an opportunity to play with a secular band, but my mom and dad wouldn't permit it. I was more into music than wrestling, so I didn't wrestle during my sophomore year in high school, and you wouldn't believe the way my family reacted. They were very upset. So I went back and wrestled my junior year."

As the end of high school neared, his parents gave Guerrero an option: He could either go to college or look for a job. Guerrero admits he was rebellious and hated being told

"I know he did that just to stop me from joining the Navy, but I went for it, and I've never regretted it. I've enjoyed every bit of my wrestling career."

what to do. He decided his quick fix would be a trip to a U.S. Navy recruitment office—yet another decision that Guerrero's parents were not ecstatic about. The day Guerrero was scheduled to take his physical and swear in, Gory pulled him into his El Paso office where he ran promotions in both Texas and Juarez, Mexico.

"Why don't you come wrestle for me, Hector?" Gory passionately pleaded from behind his desk.

"But Dad, I'm so thin!" Hector replied.

"If you don't start now, you're never going to start," Gory reasoned.

The father was right and the son knew it, questionable motivations and all. "I know he did that just to stop me from joining the Navy, but I went for it, and I've never regretted it. I've enjoyed every bit of my wrestling career."

Guerrero began training to become a professional wrestler while attending the University of Texas at El Paso (UTEP). During every Christmas break, spring break, and the ten weeks of summer vacation he would travel to Mexico City to wrestle, and during the school year he worked matches for his father in El Paso. Before he knew what was happening, Guerrero found himself hooked on the wrestling business that had now taken hold of his life. The wrestling bug had finally bitten and Guerrero's love for the ring eventually overtook his better judgment. Just before his senior year at UTEP, he defied his parents' wishes and dropped out of college.

By 1977, Guerrero had hit the independent Mexican circuit with reckless abandon. The National Wrestling Alliance (NWA) in Mexico was going through major changes, as many of its biggest stars (such as El Santo, Blue Demon, and El Solitario) were breaking away and working for various independent promotions throughout the country. Guerrero's timing couldn't have been better. He quickly landed with some of the hottest stars and was introduced as an up-and-coming talent. But as good as it was, Guerrero's success in Mexico never lived up to his high expectations. Promises of title belts and title shots were left unfulfilled, and a trip back to the U.S. became increasingly attractive as the days passed.

Chavo and Mando had already moved on to greener pastures. Chavo spent time in Texas and Florida before moving to Los Angeles where he earned the nickname "The Million Dollar Rookie." Mando had migrated farther north to San Francisco and was working in both the film industry as a stunt double and as a wrestler for such promotions as the Western States Alliance (WSA). The younger brother landed in Southern California, where he lived with Chavo. He wrestled for the Hollywood Wrestling Office (HWO), an organization run by Mike Labelle in Los Angeles. Looking to make ends meet, Guerrero was searching out additional employment opportunities when the chance of a lifetime presented itself.

Gene Labelle, a stunt man with Paramount Pictures, approached Guerrero one day at a wrestling match and told him to stop by the studios. Labelle was looking for a stunt double to work on a Tony Curtis film called *The Bad News Bears Go to Japan*, the sequel to the cult classic *The Bad News Bears*. Guerrero's wrestling background made him the perfect choice to perform Curtis' wrestling stunts while acting as "The Masked Marvel" during one of the film's action sequences.

At the same time, Guerrero's wrestling career was reaching new heights. One of his greatest opportunities came in a "battle royal," a time-honored wrestling tradition. Some of the biggest stars would gather in Los Angeles for this event, and in 1978, Guerrero was the last man standing, despite some obvious shortcomings.

"They put in little ol' Hector, one of the smallest dudes," Hector says of his surprise entry. "Everybody was so big, and I was the thinnest one. I was in shape but not as big as the others."

Guerrero earned several titles with a number of wrestling organizations. While wrestling with the HWO, he held the Americas Heavyweight Championship and participated in the World Tag Team Championship with Mando. His travels took him many places, including Oklahoma, where he snagged the Tri-States tag team belt while working for Leroy McGuirk's Tulsa-based promotion. Guerrero also gained experience with two separate stints in Japan.

Along the way, the unmarried Guerrero began living with a woman, a decision that would initiate a very turbulent time in his life. "Things were going really good for me until I met a girl," Guerrero says. He chuckles now when he talks about it, but at the time, relationships with the opposite sex became stumbling blocks in his life. Guerrero ended the first relationship after two and a half years, and would later marry and settle down with his first wife.

After touring the country with the NWA, Guerrero began to work the independent circuits and found himself in Tennessee with the Memphis Promotion and later in Knoxville with the USWA. Despite Guerrero's success in the ring, his personal life was in turmoil. Most people considered Guerrero's marriage to be a healthy one, but the relationship was strained by the ever-changing tides of the wrestling industry. The constant moving, combined with an extra-marital affair and an increasingly evident drinking problem, threatened to end their union. His life was falling apart.

Then one fateful day, Guerrero had a life-changing encounter with God. Overwhelmed by his problems and a sense of hopelessness, Guerrero lay on his couch weeping uncontrollably. Suddenly, out of nowhere, the brutish wrestler heard a still, small voice.

"I love you."

Guerrero turned around, only to find no one there. The tears returned, but once again a mysterious voice overcame his sobbing.

"I love you," the voice said again.

Deep down, Guerrero knew Who was speaking to him.

"God, forgive me of all my sins and everything that I've been doing," he prayed.

"All of a sudden I felt something go through me like lightning," Guerrero explains. "At a slow pace, it came through the top of my head, and then it went through me and almost knocked me off my feet. It felt like a beam of energy going through me."

Not long after this encounter with God, Guerrero experienced a miracle that would further impact his life in a powerful way. Having returned to Mexico to wrestle for EMLL, Guerrero suffered a crown fracture in his left heel in a match against a much smaller opponent named Negro Casas.

"I threw a dive on him, and I knew he couldn't catch me," Guerrero says. "So I bucked my heels down to lessen the impact. The pain was incredible. They said I'd never be the same again. They said I'd never be able to walk. It would hurt, and I would have to have a special shoe."

The specialist took an X-ray of his foot just before the casting process began. After they cast his foot, they took a second X-ray, but this time the fracture was closed. Confounded by the new pictures, the doctor changed his tune. "You're gonna be walking!" he told Guerrero. Throughout the next several days he spent in Mexico City, visitors were amazed to discover that his cast, predominantly cold to the touch, felt noticeably warmer along the injured heel. Just twelve and a half weeks later, Guerrero was back performing his high flying wrestling moves.

In his heart, Guerrero knew things were going to get better, but he still faced an uphill climb. Shortly after returning to the ring, his first marriage ended in divorce. But he never lost his determination to develop his relationship with God by praying and reading his Bible consistently. Doors began to open up for Guerrero to share his testimony in the most unlikely places. In fact, Guerrero has often been handed the microphone by promoters and asked to speak to the crowd.

"It's been a privilege to minister the gospel wherever I go for these independent wrestling shows," Guerrero says. "There's been too many times to count where God has given me a

Confounded by the new pictures, the doctor changed his tune. "You're gonna be walking!" he told Guerrero.

word to say and at least one person was saved. I never would have believed that people could be saved at a wrestling match."

In 1993, Guerrero returned to El Paso, Texas, to complete his degree at UTEP. While there, he would fall in love again and marry for the second time. After graduating in 1996 with a bachelor's degree in physical education, Guerrero found himself back in the national wrestling spotlight with WCW, where his brother Eddy and nephew Chavo Jr. were involved in a clever family-based angle. A feud between the two developed in June, and by July the elder Guerrero was brought in to bring the family back together. During his stint with WCW, Guerrero had the privilege of teaming with both Eddy and Chavo Jr., and also enjoyed singles matches against his younger brother. But once the feud was over, WCW and Guerrero ended their working relationship.

Unfortunately, Guerrero would again face challenges in his personal life. Despite the fact that he and his second wife had worked in ministry together, the marriage failed. The two had tried reconcil-

"Now I don't care. If God wants to do something completely different, it's OK with me."

HECTOR GUERRERO

ing, but those efforts were unsuccessful. Determined to walk on with God, Guerrero would land a job as a physical education teacher at an elementary school in Central Florida. He also developed a weight loss program that incorporates biblical principles.

Guerrero's perseverance paid off in the year 2001 with successes both inside and outside the ring. He was asked to reprise his short-lived role as the masked character "The Gobbly Gooker" at *Wrestlemania XVII* for a "gimmick battle royal." He also began working with Ted DiBiase's Power Wrestling Alliance, a promotion aimed at spreading the Gospel.

Guerrero's personal life also took a turn for the better when he reconnected with an old girlfriend named Penny. On Valentine's Day 2001, seventeen years to the day after they had ended their previous one year dating relationship, Guerrero and Penny resumed a courtship that resulted in their marriage on July 1, 2001.

Guerrero knows something big is ahead in his life, professionally, financially, personally, and spiritually. Setbacks that once might have pushed Guerrero over the edge have only served to make him stronger in his faith. The wrestler who once prayed for a second chance at wrestling glory is more concerned about what God wants him to do, regardless of financial or personal struggles that point him in other directions.

"Now I don't care," Guerrero says. "If God wants to do something completely different, it's OK with me. I heard Benny Hinn once say, 'Preach the gospel, and He'll take care of the rest.'"

Guerrero takes a deep breath and pauses for effect.

"I'm going to preach the gospel."

HECTOR GUERRERO

FULL NAME: Hector Manuel Guerrero

NICKNAMES: Lazor Tron, The Gobbly Gooker

BIRTHDATE: October 1, 1954

BIRTHPLACE: Mexico City, Mexico

HOMETOWN: Tampa, Florida

EDUCATION: University of Texas at El Paso

FAMILY: Penny (wife), Herlinda (mom), Mando, Chavo, Eddy (brothers); Cookie, Linda (sisters)

PRO WRESTLING DEBUT: 1973

FIRST MATCH: Defeated Triton Zuma in a televised match for Guerrero Resources, Inc., in Juarez, Mexico

PROMOTIONS: NWA, WCW, WWF, AWA, HWO, CWA, ECW, SMW, PWF, USWA, Mid-Atlantic Championship Wrestling, CWF, Mid-South, Tri-States, WSA, PWA

TITLES HELD: U.S./ Mexico Border Championship; America's Heavyweight; America's Tag Team; HWO World Tag Team (w/ Mando); NWA Tri-States Tag Team; NWA U.S. Tag Team; NWA Florida Heavyweight; Mid-South Tag Team; AWA Southern Tag Team; NWA World Junior Heavyweight

WORST INJURY: Crown fracture to the heel

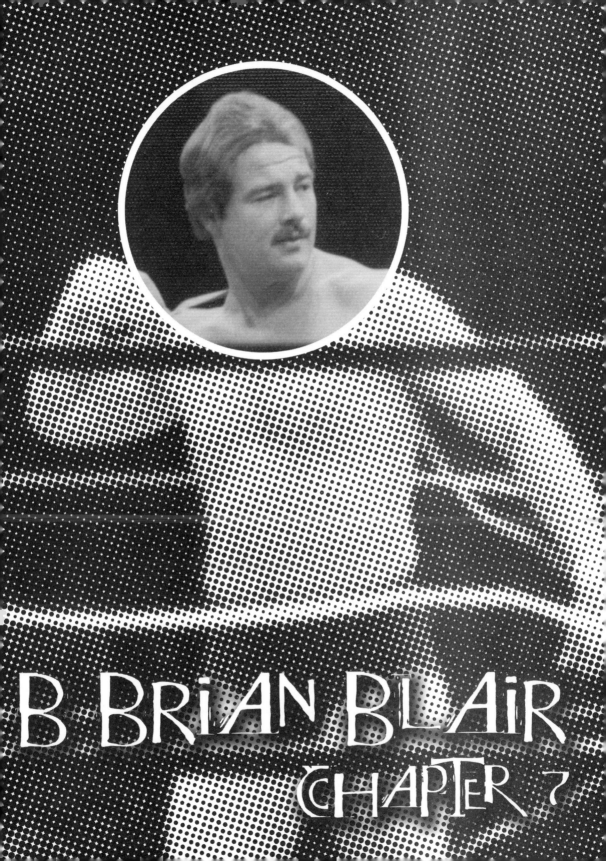

B BRIAN BLAIR

CHAPTER 7

B BRIAN BLAIR

CHAPTER 7

For as long as B Brian Blair can remember, he wanted to be Superman. He talked about it, dreamed about it, and even prayed about it. For fifteen years, Blair did everything in his power to make that dream come true. At the impressionable age of seven, Blair began developing a childlike faith in God that was fortified by the words of his mother and a certain Lutheran pastor. There was one message in particular that stirred the little guy's imagination and drove him to his knees.

"The pastor was talking about the power of prayer," Blair recalls. "So I prayed and hoped that someday I would be Superman, because he was my hero. Actually, God did answer my prayer, because to me a professional wrestler is about as close as you can get to Superman. You're a fictitious character, you get to dress up in a costume, and you act like you're a lot stronger than you really are."

Born January 12 in Gary, Indiana but raised in nearby Aetna, Blair was the oldest of four children. His father was a carpenter and held two jobs, while his mother stayed at home with the children. When Blair was eleven years old, his father moved the family to Tampa, Florida, to pursue a better job opportunity. At that point, Blair's parents were already experiencing marital problems, although the children rarely saw them argue. Two years later they reached an "agreeable separation" that led to divorce. Despite the unfortunate circumstances of his childhood, Blair maintains a wonderful relationship with both of his parents to this day.

Blair and his siblings found themselves on the move from apartment to apartment for the better part of five years. Their mother did her best to support the family with her estranged hus-

For as long as B Brian Blair can remember, he wanted to be Superman.

band's help, but when he was laid off, things got even tougher. With no income for three months, the Blair family had to rely on any means necessary to survive.

"I was waiting in line, and I had these food stamps," Blair says. "I was kind of embarrassed, because I knew that wasn't a cool thing. Sure enough, just when I get ready to pay the lady, three kids from school come in behind me. They see me giving the lady food stamps, and these three kids told the whole school that I was poor, and they called me some pretty bad names. There were a lot of nights of tears. Even then, I felt like God was watching over me."

At the age of sixteen, Blair moved out, sharing a house with four others, all older than he was. Blair held a number of odd jobs that helped him pay his share of the monthly rent and buy food. Blair ran a newspaper route, welded mailbox posts, worked in a Kmart shoe department, and sold sodas at the University of Tampa football games. There, he watched his heroes, Paul Orndorff and Freddy Solomon, play for the home team. Orndorff and Blair's paths would cross again a few years later.

"I thought wrestling was real then. I really believed it was a shoot. I knew I was going to have to be a tough guy to be a wrestler. So I played football, and I wrestled."

With what money Blair had left each week, he would purchase a ticket to the Tuesday night wrestling match at the armory. Blair was crazy about professional wrestling and rarely missed a night of action. "I thought wrestling was real then," Blair says. "I really believed it was a shoot. I knew I was going to have to be a tough guy to be a wrestler. So I played football, and I wrestled."

During his senior year at Tampa Bay Tech, Blair had an award-winning football season. College recruiters came calling on the young athlete, known for his intense hustle and big heart. Blair accepted an offer to play for the University of Tampa, where he hoped to follow in Orndorff's footsteps. Those plans changed, however, when the school abruptly terminated its football program after his freshman year. Instead, Blair would spend a semester at St. Leo's College in Dade City, Florida, before transferring to the University of Louisville in Kentucky.

Blair loved football. But by the end of the 1977 season, he was pining for home. That summer, he rushed back to learn the ins and outs of professional wrestling. Blair began training with legendary Japanese wrestler Hiro Matsuda at the Sportatorium in Tampa, home of Eddie Graham's Florida Championship Wrestling offices.

The first few days would represent one of the most physically trying times of his life. His body would be stretched, beaten, bruised, and stretched even more. Matsuda was a master at cleaning house and ridding the program of underachievers. In fact, he usually needed only one day to do so. But Blair was different. The first two days of Matsuda's torture resulted in Blair vomiting at the end of each session. The youngster was embarrassed but remained determined. In order to rectify the problem, Blair decided not to eat between workouts. The plan succeeded and caused Matsuda to ask questions.

"Why you don't throw up today?" Matsuda asked. "What's the matter? Why you don't throw up?"

"I haven't eaten since yesterday at noon," Blair replied.

Blair's answer yielded a hearty laugh from Matsuda, who then took Blair under his wings and became an instant supporter of the young wrestler's career. One summer later, it was a young Terry Bollea (better known as Hulk Hogan) who entered the Sportatorium. Blair and Hogan struck up a friendship that continues to

Blair was off to Kansas City, Missouri . . . There, he crossed paths with another future WWF star, Jesse Ventura. The two worked together for what Blair described as "eight months of misery."

this day. At the time, Hogan played bass and sang backup vocals for a local rock band called Ruckus. Blair would sneak into the clubs to see his buddy entertain. Even then, Blair saw a star in the making.

By the beginning of 1978, Blair had worked more than sixty matches, but Hogan was just getting started. In what was Hogan's second match, the two hooked up as part of a card that included Jack and Gerald Briscoe. Hogan wore a black mask and performed as a bad guy called The Destroyer. The fight was scheduled to go to a twenty-minute "broadway" or to a draw. Unfortunately for Blair and Hogan, the Briscoes had something else in mind.

"We had our entire repertoire set up, and we did everything we knew that we could possibly do in twenty minutes," Blair explains. "We were both so tired we could hardly stand it, and we were just waiting for that twenty minutes to come. When it was supposed to be twenty minutes, the bell didn't ring. Instead, the announcer said, 'Twenty minutes gone, ten minutes to go.' It was terrible. We actually went an extra ten minutes, and I'm sure it was horrible. When we got to the dressing room, the Briscoes were back there laughing hysterically at our expense."

After attending the University of Louisville and cutting his teeth in Florida with the Briscoes, Blair was off to Kansas City, Missouri, and Bob Geigel's Central States promotion. There, he crossed paths with another future WWF star, Jesse Ventura. The two worked together for what Blair described as "eight months of misery." Kansas City was notorious among wrestlers as one of their least favorite territories, but Blair and Ventura made it work. Blair remembers one particular main event match with Ventura that didn't end so pleasantly.

Once again Blair was the babyface, while Ventura took on the role of heel. The two hit the ring in front of a packed house and prepared for a battle. Blair landed his first blow to Ventura's head, and the crowd immediately roared with approval. Blair continued his onslaught while Ventura simply took the beating until a mere two minutes had passed. Before the two knew it, Blair had driven Ventura all the way to the backstage area. Unfortunately for the two wrestlers, that was not what bookers Pat O'Connor and Bob Geigel were expecting.

"They never told us that [Ventura] was supposed to stop me so we could have a regular match," Blair says. "We took the biggest chewing-out from Pat O'Connor and Bob Geigel that we'd ever heard."

Blair's next stop was Tulsa, Oklahoma, where he worked for Leroy McGuirk's Tri-States promotion. In 1979, Blair quickly rose to main event status. That year, he won one of his first major titles by defeating Ron Starr in Springfield, Missouri, for the Junior Heavyweight title. But during his stay in Tulsa, Blair also made two of the biggest mistakes of his life.

Upon arrival, he was quickly warned to stay away from McGuirk's young and very attractive daughter Michael. Mixing romance with business was never a good idea, yet Blair proceeded hastily and aggressively. It wasn't long before the two were dating, and within a year, the couple had exchanged wedding vows. By Blair's own account, the union was doomed from the start. "She was around the business, and that was a tough situation," Blair says. "When you're young, sometimes you have to learn things the hard way."

While in Tulsa, Blair befriended another young wrestler named Doug Summers. The pair found themselves hanging out together most of the time. But the friendship suffered a major blow when Blair started to hear rumors that Summers was having an affair with his now-estranged wife. Blair and Michael were already nearing divorce when the situation came to blows. It was Blair's last night in Tulsa before he was to leave for Dallas, where the Von Erichs had requested his services.

"I was in the office, and all of a sudden Doug Summers walked in," Blair recalls. "I wasn't sure if him and Michael were having an affair, but I had heard that they were. He looked at me, and I just couldn't stand it, so I hit him. I hurt him really bad. There was blood all over the office, and some of Leroy's pictures were broken."

Still fuming from the confrontation, Blair failed to assess the damage. After making final preparations to leave town, Blair collected his thoughts and decided to tell his soon-to-be ex-wife goodbye. He knocked on the door, only to have the legally blind Leroy McGuirk answer the door.

"Who is it?" McGuirk inquired.

"It's Brian. I want to talk to Michael."

McGuirk verbally assaulted Blair with a colorful array of expletives, sending the guilty son-in-law back to his car. After what seemed like two hours, Blair braved a second trip back to the front door, hoping for a better result.

Once again, McGuirk answered the door.

"Who is it?" McGuirk asked again.

"It's Brian," Blair replied.

After a long pause, the door finally opened, only to reveal McGuirk equipped with a handgun. He opened the screen door and lifted the gun from

"God was working in my life, and I knew He had a plan for my life. I wasn't ready to accept all of the things that came with that yet, but I believed and I had faith and I always said my prayers."

his side. Blair had to think fast. He quickly ducked behind the brickwork on the front of the house. A resounding "boom!" shot through the air. Blair could see the bullet hitting beneath the front tire of McGuirk's own Lincoln Continental. Unsure of his father-in-law's intentions—did he want to hurt him or simply scare him away?—Blair waited safely out of gunfire range as his heart rate skyrocketed. Blair bravely decided to take one last chance.

"I went around to the back of the house to see if I could find

Michael," Blair says. "I looked in the window, and there was a guy who looked like a mummy lying on the couch. His face was all covered up, and there were just holes for two eyes and a mouth. It was Doug Summers, and Michael was feeding some soup to him. That really crushed my heart. I drove all the way to Dallas that night. I cried a lot and thought a lot. It was a tough time."

In Texas, the legendary Von Erich family welcomed Blair into their lives with open arms. It was just the environment he needed to help heal his self-inflicted wounds. Fritz Von Erich led the business and would routinely add an extra $100 to Blair's check. He never charged Blair rent during the time he stayed with David, one of his five sons. Blair was gaining momentum in the ring, but more importantly, he was starting to realize the importance of his faith. He found strength in a Bible given to him by Kerry Von Erich. "I felt the Spirit of God growing in me," Blair says. "God was working in my life, and I knew He had a plan for my life. I wasn't ready to accept all of the things that came with that yet, but I believed and I had faith and I always said my prayers."

Tragically, all but one of the Von Erich brothers would pass away, though long after Blair had left. Three suicides and a fatal wrestling injury would leave Kevin the sole surviving Von Erich. Looking back at his time in Texas is sobering and reminds Blair of how thankful he is just to be alive. "Half of my friends that I grew up with are dead," Blair says. "When you put your faith in the Lord and know that somebody else is looking out for your life, your life's not totally in your hands. You're given enough wisdom to make good choices, and hopefully you'll make those choices. But God has a plan for your life."

After a brief return to Florida, Blair received his first call from New York. At that time, Vince McMahon Sr. was running the show for the World Wide Wrestling Federation (WWWF). Blair was sent to Japan, where he worked for New Japan Wrestling. His fondest memories include classic matches against Antonio Inoki and Tatsumi Fujinami. Blair also recalls the long train ride he took every Sunday to services at a Catholic church, the closest house of worship he could find.

On July 11, 1982, Blair made a triumphant return to his home state by defeating Jimmy Garvin for the Florida State Heavyweight championship. His stay didn't last long. Vince McMahon Jr. had taken over for his ailing father (who later died of prostate cancer) and was ready to expand to the national promotion that he renamed the World Wrestling Federation (WWF).

In 1983, Blair moved on to Georgia Championship Wrestling under the direction of Jim Barnett. With a strong connection to Turner Broadcasting Systems (TBS), the Georgia promotion received a good deal of television exposure, unlike anything Blair had experienced before. He also had the privilege of working with the likes of Tony Atlas, Tito Santana, the Freebirds, and Paul Orndorff.

Blair stayed in Atlanta for a year before heading back to

Florida, where he enjoyed continued success. His highlights included a Southern Championship title over Ravishing Rick Rude and a regaining of the Florida Heavyweight belt against Jesse Barr. It was in Florida that he received an unexpected phone call from his longtime friend Hogan. He wanted to know if Blair had heard of an up-and-coming American Wrestling Association (AWA) star named Jumpin' Jim Brunzell. George Scott, head booker for the WWF, was courting the two for a tag team he was hoping to form. Blair and Brunzell met up with Scott in New York to discuss the possibilities.

The duo hit if off immediately, and suddenly the team was working on an image and name. At the time, the Miami Dolphins football team had a portion of its defensive unit nicknamed "The Killer B's," and Blair suggested that maybe that name could be reshaped to fit him and Brunzell. It so happened that Lanny Poffo had some black and yellow "bee" tights, and the Killer Bees were born.

"We started at *Wrestlemania II* in 1985," Blair recalls. "Orndorff was on the first *Wrestlemania*. It's funny how I always followed him from territory to territory. We had a tremendous run. They had Mr. T as our manager, and they made a big deal out of that. Then came the Hart Foundation. We had a huge feud with them."

Blair can't remember how many matches the Killer Bees fought against Bret "The Hitman" Hart and Jim "The Anvil" Neidhart, but he does remember gaining an enormous amount of respect for

Hart. Years later, he would name his first son after the wrestling legend. "I added an extra 't' to give it an Americanized spelling," Blair jokingly says. "I always liked Bret. I had to like him after working with him so much."

From 1985 to 1988, wrestling was reaching its greatest heights. It was the first true mainstream boom, and Blair was reaping the benefits and simultaneously feeling the strain. At one point, Blair and Brunzell were on the road for sixty-seven days without a break. Both men reached breaking points but collectively found strength in their faith.

"The business is tough," Blair says. "One time during that road stretch, he was crying on the phone, and he was miserable. I tried to comfort him. We had to make money, and that's how we made money. It was such a sacrifice. I can see how if he hadn't had Christ too, he could have really slipped off the deep end. It was nice, because a lot of times we would pray together."

Other frustrations resulted from negative business decisions. Although the Killer Bees went on to work *Wrestlemania III* and *IV*, unfulfilled promises and dissatisfaction led to the end of Blair's rope with the WWF. Just before *Wrestlemania V*, the situation reached its boiling point. "They promised us the titles, and we never got them," Blair says. "It really made me mad. It was very disappointing, because the belts did mean something."

"We're not happy anymore," Blair told Vince McMahon Jr.

"If you're not happy," he replied, "then there's no sense in you being around."

Blair was glad for the break. He was burned out on the business and felt the need to search out other opportunities. Little did Blair know that his greatest successes were yet to come. While still in the WWF, his old wrestling coach set him up on a blind date. Coach Lloyd and his wife waited with the young woman at Lirello's Restaurant until Blair arrived.

Blair walked in and spotted the older couple, but his eyes were quickly diverted to the beautiful blonde-haired girl sitting with them.

"*Wow*," Blair thought. His face radiated with interest in the woman, named Toni. Blair and Toni dated for a year after that initial meeting before tying the knot and settling down in Tampa. They waited several years before they welcomed Brett (born in 1992) and Bradley (born in 1995) into the world. Having a family was the fulfillment of a lifelong dream as well as an answered prayer. Blair finally had the perfect family he had always longed for, complete with his own set of "Killer B's."

After leaving the WWF, Blair returned to Florida, where he continued to wrestle. He also made his way back to Japan, where he continued to work until 1995. In that year, World Championship Wrestling (WCW) took over booking for New Japan Wrestling, leaving Blair out in the cold. By 1990, wrestling was no longer the source of income it once had been, and it was time to start planning for the future. "I had $80,000 in the bank, and I knew that wasn't enough to carry me very far," Blair says. "I needed to do something. I decided to start a gym, and I thought if I was going to start a gym, it might as well be a Gold's Gym."

In 1990, Blair opened his first fitness facility in Tampa. Hogan's special appearance at the grand opening created a line of people that stretched a half-mile long. That first year, Blair's gym grossed $125,000, and soon a second franchise followed. For the next eight years, Blair successfully ran three Gold's Gyms, which employed as many as ninety people at a time. Blair was personally making $100,000 a year, and the two gyms were grossing a combined $3 million a year.

Blair fully believes that his overwhelming rise in the fitness industry is due to his strong belief in prayer, but after spending the better part of the 1990s stressed out over business operations, his prayers addressed an entirely different problem. "There came a point in my life where all of a sudden I would be getting phone calls at three o'clock in the morning," Blair says. "Everybody had my number, and if the gym didn't open up at six o'clock, I'd have twenty calls. I didn't think I could take it anymore. It was so stressful.

"I went to this room, and I got on my knees for seven nights," Blair remembers. "With tears in my eyes, I prayed, 'Dear God, You promised me You wouldn't give me a burden that I couldn't bear. I can't bear this anymore. Father, please help me.'"

On the seventh day of his routine, Blair received a phone call from a man looking to purchase his gyms. Oddly enough, Blair's gyms were not on the market. He had not uttered a single word to anyone about his struggles. The next day, he received another phone call from a second man also looking to buy his gyms.

"The first guy was moving into town with a new fitness concept, and he knew that I had a lock on the market," Blair explains. "The second guy had opened up a gym in South Tampa. So the two guys got into a bidding war, and I wound up selling my gyms in a multi-million-dollar deal. If that's not a testimony to the power of prayer, then I don't know what is."

"I've got a lot of trophies at my house. I have a lot of awards and things like that. But the only trophies that I'll ever take to Heaven are those [people] tha I lead to Christ."

For now, Blair is unsure of how wrestling will play into his future. In December 1999, Shane McMahon (Vince Jr.'s son) approached Blair about working for the WWF, but his request to work only half of the year killed the deal. He has notebooks full of characters and storyline developments and would love to get back into the business as a writer or a consultant. In 2000, Blair wrote a book called *Smarten Up* that dissects much of the lingo used in the business and demystifies the tricks of the trade used by wrestling insiders. While remaining active with his local church, Blair has also been encouraged by friends and others in the Tampa area to run for political office.

The only other way he knows how to squelch the wrestling bug is to hit the ring four or five times a month. Each time, as he pulls on the tights and laces up the boots, B Brian Blair becomes that fabled comic book legend once again. As for the rest of his time, he becomes Superman to his two boys, his wife, and hundreds of school kids and young athletes throughout the community. Still young and full of energy, Blair has accomplished much, but with God's help, he plans to do even more.

"Here I am," Blair reflects. "I'm looking out the back of my house to a beautiful lake. I've got nice cars and material things. But most of all, above all, I have faith and family. Those are the greatest things in the world. I've got a lot of trophies at my house. I have a lot of awards and things like that. But the only trophies that I'll ever take to Heaven are those [people] that I lead to Christ."

B BRIAN BLAIR

FULL NAME: Brian Leslie Blair

NICKNAMES: B; Killer Bee

BIRTHDATE: January 12

BIRTHPLACE: Gary, Indiana

HOMETOWN: Tampa, Florida

EDUCATION: Undergraduate Studies at Tampa Bay Tech, St. Leo's College, and the University of Louisville

HEIGHT: 6'3"

WEIGHT: 230 lbs.

FAMILY: Toni (wife); Brett, Bradley (sons)

PRO WRESTLING DEBUT: Summer of 1978, The Sportatorium (Tampa, Florida)

FIRST MATCH: Pat Patterson & Ivan Koloff defeated B Brian Blair & Skip Young

PROMOTIONS: WWF, WWWF, WCW, FCW, Mid-South, Georgia Championship Wrestling, Central States, NWA, World Class Wrestling

TITLES HELD: FCW Heavyweight, Southern Heavyweight, Central States Tag Team, World Junior Heavyweight, Asia Pacific Heavyweight, Americas Tag Team

FINISHING MOVES: Boston Crab, Sleeper Hold

BEST FEUDS: Singles vs. Paul Orndorff, Jesse Barr; Tag Team with Jim Brunzell (the Killer Bees) vs. The Hart Foundation (Bret Hart & Jim "The Anvil" Neidhart)

WORST INJURY: Tendons in his right hand snapped during a match in Japan requiring over 300 stitches

BRUNO SASSI
CHAPTER 8

BRUNO SASSI

CHAPTER 8

n the world of high-stakes professional wrestling, there's a set way of doing things. Clichés such as food chain, totem pole, and pecking order certainly work well in describing the business. First there are the main event superstars like The Rock, Steve Austin, Bill Goldberg, and Hulk Hogan. Then there are the mid-carders, highly popular athletes like Chris Jericho, Dean Malenko, Billy Kidman, and Rey Misterio Jr. who are still reaching for the top. Just below them, there's another rung or two on the ladder, occupied by a multitude of talent either on their way up or on their way down and out.

Then there are the Bruno Sassis of the world. "I lay on the mat on my back and let people count me out," Sassi jokingly says.

Affectionately known as "jobbers" due to their willingness to "do the job," they take more punishment than they give, lose more than they win, and see just enough television time to turn the occasional head while walking down the street. Sassi has made a career out of losing to some of the best wrestlers in the business. Mick Foley (a.k.a. Mankind), Jeff Jarrett, Billy Gunn, Brian

Christopher, Hugh Morrus, Dave Heath (a.k.a. Gangrel), Stevie Richards, and Public Enemy are just a few opponents who have marked a "W" next to Sassi's name in their record books. And he's loved every single match.

"I'm an extra," Sassi says. "And that's fine. Whatever the role is, I don't mind. I understand how things are."

Sassi wasn't always so tolerant of the concept. From a very early age, he dreamed of achieving professional wrestling glory. His Italian father, Francesco (Frank), and Peruvian mother, Teresa, met when Teresa was on a summer trip in Europe. Later, the couple would renew their friendship in Peru, where Frank was stationed during his military service. They married and opened a café in Peru. After the birth of their first son, Francesco, they moved to Baltimore, Maryland, where Bruno was born in 1970.

Sassi has made a career out of losing to some of the best wrestlers in the business. . . . And he's loved every single match.

Sassi remembers little about Baltimore, mostly just Orioles baseball and the wrestling matches he faithfully watched on television. By the time Sassi was five, the family had moved to

BRUNO SASSI

Hollywood, Florida, a suburb of Fort Lauderdale, where his parents started a business. Like most Italian families Sassi knew, his was Catholic. Their inconsistent church attendance, however, left Sassi with an empty feeling. "It was total ritual," Sassi says. "There was no relationship with God. It was dead. There was nothing there."

In Florida, Sassi developed a taste for athletics by playing baseball, football, and throwing the shot-put and discus for the track and field team. He attended Miramar High School, where his participation in amateur wrestling was short-lived. "I just went out to have fun, and this

"It was a fast lesson in life as I watched him deteriorate. In a matter of six months, I'd grown up and become a man."

guy decided to get cute with me," Sassi recalls. "He rolled back the tape on his wrists and started rubbing it on my eyes. So from watching wrestling all my life, I just picked him up and dropped him on his head. That was the end of my [amateur] wrestling career."

Back at home, his family was experiencing troublesome times with the discovery of Francesco's health problems. A long-time cigarette smoker, he was diagnosed with lung cancer. At age sixteen, Sassi stared hard at the prospects of losing his father. For the next six months, Sassi spent most of his days at his father's side. Still in high school and working a part-time job, he somehow found the time to feed, change, bathe, and do everything else for his father. "It was a fast lesson in life as I watched him deteriorate," Sassi says. "In a matter of six months, I'd grown up and become a man. I don't think that my family understood that I was no longer a boy."

Frank Sassi would pass away on Christmas Day of 1987 at the age of sixty-five. Sassi's first big decision without his father came in September of 1988. His choice to become a professional wrestler was met with a collective groan of disapproval. Instead of accepting the multitude of scholarships available to him, Sassi entered Broward Community College and began learning the wrestling ropes under the tutelage of Rusty Brooks. The accomplished instructor had previously partnered with Boris Malenko (father of WWF wrestler Dean Malenko) at the Global Wrestling Alliance and now ran the Independent Professional Wrestling Association (IPWA).

Seventeen years old and barely out of high school, Sassi began his training on September 10, 1988. For the next twenty days he learned the moves, took the bumps, and toughened up for the ring. Sassi's first opportunity came sooner than expected when one of Brooks' wrestlers took a show in Calgary for Stu Hart and was unable to make it back to Florida in time.

"Bruno, I have an open spot," Rusty told his young hopeful. "Do you think you can do it?"

"Of course I can do it," Sassi nervously responded with a crack in his voice.

Sassi admits he wasn't prepared for the match that night. His opponent, dressed in a sheik-like outfit, won the match, but Sassi is thankful for the consideration that was shown him. "The match wasn't too bad," Sassi says. "The guy I was wrestling with helped me out. He didn't kill me in there. I did what I was supposed to do, and we had a pretty good time that night."

For the next two years, Sassi took every show he could. He didn't care how much it paid or if it paid at all. If he had a shot to get into a ring and wrestle, he would find a way to get there. He and his wrestling accomplices would sometimes drive as much as fourteen hours for nothing but gas money. "It was ridiculous what we would do to get to these places," Sassi says.

Sassi teamed up with Dan Ackerman and Dave Heath to form the Bad Boys, a gang gimmick that didn't exactly fit. Heath would go on to become known as Gangrel in the WWF during a run in the late 1990s. Slowly but surely, Sassi climbed the local wrestling ladder and emerged as one of the scene's star commodities. Alcohol, drugs, and sexual promiscuity were nightly temptations. Sassi was signing autographs and living the life of a local hero. When he went back home each night, he was still the kid brother who had no business making any decisions on his own. "Being pushed out by my family was kind of hard," Sassi says. "That was when I needed them to be there for me the most. So I got rebellious. I wasn't an alcoholic or a drug addict, but if I wanted to drink, I'd drink. If I wanted to smoke pot, I'd smoke pot. I didn't go out and buy it all the time. Usually friends just brought stuff over and I'd join them, just fitting in."

For the next three years, Sassi aggressively worked the Florida independent circuit. He credits Eddie Mansfield for giving him his first big break in the business. Mansfield ran the International Wrestling Federation (IWF) out of Orlando, where he both promoted shows and wrestled. The IWF was regularly televised on a sports cable station that could be seen throughout the state. Sassi had already made his first national television appearance working for the National Wrestling Alliance (NWA) in a 1990 match against the late Brian Pillman. Mansfield started sending tapes of his televised wrestling matches to all parts of the world. That led to a run in Puerto Rico, where Sassi and his teammates worked for the World Wrestling Council (WWC) and even held the world tag team belts for a short time.

"Now we were the world tag team title holders, and ego came into play," Sassi admits. "We were young and stupid. We didn't know anything except we were there having a good time and I was starting to fit in. It was great. So what was the next step? We were going to make millions."

WRESTLING WITH GOD

It was a hard, cold reality check when Sassi returned to Florida. Expecting the phone to ring off the hook with offers from the major promotions, Sassi and his friends were quickly brought back down to earth. Instead of making it big, they had to look for jobs and settle back into the routine of everyday life. Sassi spent the next eight months recovering from five broken ribs he received in Puerto Rico. Still stinging from his father's death, his

family's lack of support, and the uncertainty of his wrestling career, Sassi took his frustrations out on God.

"I was upset with God," Sassi says. "I fought with God. I would say

"I was upset with God. I fought with God. I would say 'You don't exist!' But I knew He did, because I would talk to Him. I was struggling inside. I felt alone in the world."

'You don't exist!' But I knew He did, because I would talk to Him. I was struggling inside. I felt alone in the world."

By 1993, Sassi was working on a new gimmick. He and new partner James Tilquist debuted the Phi Delta Slam tag team in Memphis while working for the United States Wrestling Alliance (USWA). What started as an attempt to rally support for underpaid, misused wrestlers and form a fraternity of sorts turned into Sassi and company's next big gig. Sassi originally took on the name "D-Day" but eventually decided to use his real name, while Tilquist became known as "Bluto." Like Tilquist, future members of the group would take their monikers from the classic movie, *Animal House*. With little preparation and a clouded frame of mind, Sassi didn't perform well. Phi Delta Slam was sent home after just one month of ring action.

Back in Florida, Sassi met a wrestling hopeful named Andre Jimenez, who approached the five-year ring veteran for personal training. Jimenez, a recent convert to the Christian faith, wasted little time in sharing his experience with Sassi. By December, the constant witnessing was wearing Sassi down.

"Bruno, why don't you just come to church with me?" Jimenez pleaded.

"Andre, if you tell me one more time, we're gonna go at it!" Sassi threatened. "I'm telling you no!"

"Why don't you just consider it?" Jimenez asked.

"Fine!" Sassi spouted. "I'll go. But you'll never ask me again. This is it."

The following Sunday, Sassi honored his word and stepped through the doors of the Greater Miami Church of God. He remembers everything about that morning-most importantly, the sermon that was preached. It was the Old Testament story of

Joseph, who had been cast out by his brothers and sold into slavery, and how God raised him up to be a leader in Egypt and eventually allowed him the chance to rescue those same brothers from famine.

"That message was mine," Sassi says. "Everything out of that pastor's mouth was for me. The Lord crushed my heart. The Lord set me free that day and saved my soul."

"That message was mine. Everything out of that pastor's mouth was for me. The Lord crushed my heart. The Lord set me free that day and saved my soul."

Everything changed for Sassi. While he admits he didn't change overnight from the wild man he had been, there were evident differences in his life. The alcohol, drugs, and sexual excess came to a screeching halt. His wrestling career started to pick up. In June of 1994, Sassi received a call from the WWF. He and Tilquist hadn't pitched their services in more than a year, so the tryout request came as a complete surprise. The tag team didn't get the job they were hoping for but did wrestle two events for the promotion in Poughkeepsie, New York, and at Penn State University, both as part of televised events. Ever since, Sassi has routinely worked for the WWF in both dark matches (non-televised) and for shows such as

Jakked and *Metal.* He saw action for Extreme Championship Wrestling (ECW) as well, a relationship that started in Philadelphia on that same trip for WWF. Similar opportunities with World Championship Wrestling (WCW) were also offered but ultimately fizzled out before either could work a match.

By then, Sassi had started working in the ministry. He was attending Hollywood First Assembly of God, a church that had recently merged with the Italian Assembly of God under Pastor Antonio Zotti. Sassi felt that he was supposed to learn from Zotti and eventually became the full-time youth pastor, a position he holds today. Changes in his personal life were also around the corner. Sassi reintroduced himself to Angela Napoli, a childhood acquaintance from their parents' mutual involvement in the restaurant business. The two became close friends over the next six months and finally decided they were meant to be together. On May 10, 1997, Sassi married Angela. Three years later, the couple would welcome son Joseph into the world.

During Sassi's engagement, things began changing in his wrestling career as well. He was working more singles matches and found himself torn between youth ministry and the ring. He considered quitting wrestling and focusing all of his energies on the church. In 1996, he had one last match, scheduled in North Carolina for the WWF. Before he left home, he had determined that this would be his last match. Sassi spent most of the long, arduous drive praying, singing, and praying some more.

BRUNO SASSI

"Lord, I know You're not cruel," Sassi told God. "So if You don't want me in this, take my desire away completely, and I'll gladly give it up. But if You do have a work for me, then give me a double portion of desire."

As soon as he arrived at the arena, he felt something build up inside of him. It was that familiar rush of adrenaline that always came just before a match. The passion and desire to wrestle that night grew as he walked from the locker room to the walkway. When he hit the ring, he could clearly sense God telling him, "Don't stop doing this."

"I'm still in it, because it affects kids. Whenever God pulls me out, I'm out. When He says 'that's it,' and the desire's gone, I'll walk away from it."

Since that night, Sassi's bookings have doubled, and he has managed to successfully balance his wrestling career, his youth ministry, and his family life. Nearly every time the WWF comes to the National Car Rental Center in Fort Lauderdale, fans will see Bruno Sassi in a warm-up match or as part of a television taping for one of the syndicated TV shows. But no matter how bad a beating his body takes, Sassi always makes it to church the following Sunday morning. Later that week, he can be found teaching his teenage disciples how to apply biblical virtues to their lives.

"I'm still in it, because it affects kids," Sassi says of his continued wrestling career. "Whenever God pulls me out, I'm out. When He says 'that's it,' and the desire's gone, I'll walk away from it. If I never get a contract, then that's fine. I can't push God. If He wants me to stay small and share the gospel with the locals, then that's great. If He takes me to the WWF to talk to multitudes, then that's fine too. I love Christ with all my heart. I'm living for Him."

BRUNO SASSI

FULL NAME: Bruno Sassi

NICKNAMES: D-Day, Brother Bruno, Bruno Dunamis, Fraternity Brother Ace

BIRTHDATE: December 15, 1970

BIRTHPLACE: Baltimore, Maryland

HOMETOWN: Hollywood, Florida

EDUCATION: Miramar High School; Undergraduate Studies at Broward Community College and Berean University

HEIGHT: 5'10"

WEIGHT: 250 lbs.

FAMILY: Angela (wife); Joseph (son)

PRO WRESTLING DEBUT: September 30th, 1988

FIRST MATCH: As the Assassin (masked) lost to a "Sheik" character

PROMOTIONS: WWF, ECW, NWA, PWF (Pro Wrestling of Florida), USWA, WWC, JPWA, JWF, FCW, FWJ, WWW, WXO, FWO

TITLES HELD: JPWA World Tag Team, FCW World Tag Team, FWJ World Tag Team, WWW World Tag Team, WWC World Tag Team

FINISHING MOVES: Singles: The loaded boot; Tag Team: The Initiation (Sassi holds down opponent while partner performs either a moonsault or leg drop from the top rope)

BEST FEUD: vs. Dynamite Express (1993-94)

WORST INJURY: Cracked neck; broke five ribs on his left side; dislocated jaw; multiple concussions

IVAN KOLOFF

CHAPTER 9

iVAN KOLOFF

CHAPTER 9

t was hard enough for some of professional wrestling's strongest men to get him to the mat. What made Terrance Rose think he could do the trick? Ivan Koloff was still wondering how he managed to get from the back of Faith Covenant Church to the front so fast. Only a handful made it to the prayer line quicker then he did, and now he stood waiting for Rose to pray for him. The former British soccer star and wealthy business-man turned international evangelist had an average athletic build but was nowhere close to the size of Koloff's smallest ring oppo-nent.

Ivan Koloff had not responded to the altar call looking for fire-works. He just wanted a change in his life, and after soaking up Rose's testimony, Koloff knew this was something he needed. He had shown up that night on a whim while driving home from an autograph session. Now he stood with his back turned to the crowd of more than three thousand. Not concerned with what anyone was thinking, Koloff was busy noticing those beside him who were falling flat on their backs. "I knew that [pro wrestler] Animal could knock me down with a clothesline," Koloff recalls thinking. "But I couldn't picture myself doing that. I felt bad for the preacher, because I knew I wasn't going down."

By this time, Koloff's former tag team partner Nikita Koloff had slipped in behind him. It was Nikita who had asked his wrestling "uncle" to attend the church service. Both he and Rose started praying for Koloff. Less than thirty seconds later, Ivan's knees began to buckle, and he felt his body being pushed backwards, not by a man, but by an unseen force. "There was nothing I could do to stop it," Koloff says. "The Lord let me know that He was for real."

It had taken Koloff more than fifty years to come to that realization. Born in Nation Valley River, Ontario on August 25, 1942, he was the sixth of ten children. He changed his name legally from Jim Perras during this wrestling career. The myth that he was born in Russia somehow took on a life of its own. Koloff's family lived on a dairy farm and didn't have much in the way of material goods. His only athletic outlet was playing hockey with his brothers on the frozen pond and practicing wrestling moves on them.

"I fell in love with wrestling at a very young age," Koloff says. "I was eight or nine years old. We didn't have a TV at home. We were a very low-income family. We didn't have a car until later on, but we managed to get to the neighbors a few miles away. They had a TV, and I started watching wrestling there. From the first time I watched wrestling, I fell in love with it. I knew that's what I wanted to be. The dream stuck with me."

Koloff fell onto hard times at an early age. He dropped out of high school and had several run-ins with the law. Koloff spent time in jail for stealing and other petty crimes. It was his season of sowing oats, and despite the ramifications, he never truly learned his lesson. Koloff moved to Hamilton, Ontario, where he met Jack Wentworth, a former British Empire wrestling champion.

Wentworth ran a wrestling training camp and instantly saw potential in Koloff's burly frame. At eighteen years old, he weighed 183 pounds with virtually no fat on his body. Before Koloff could start his training, Wentworth wanted to help him develop his strength.

"There was nothing I could do to stop it. The Lord let me know that He was for real."

After six months of weightlifting, the young Canadian weighed 230 pounds and could bench press more than three hundred pounds. In the meantime, Koloff, along with his younger brother, worked for the steel company in town. Once Koloff was physically ready, Wentworth decided to start working with him in the ring. But first, he needed to see some ringside wrestling action. "The night before they were supposed to start training me, they had a show that [Wentworth] put on," Koloff recalls. "They charged people a dollar to get in, and they'd put 150 to 200 people in this gym. Jack Wentworth and a police officer who was a wrestler were a tag team against Sailor Clark, a guy who looked something like me, with the bald head, and Al Bell, a guy about 350 pounds, 6 foot 4."

Koloff and his younger brother watched with anticipation as the match began. Much to Koloff's dismay, Clark and Bell began double-teaming Wentworth and beating up his trainer and mentor. Koloff became so excited he barely remembers poking his brother in the arm and calling him to action.

"Let's get 'em!" Koloff yelled.

He ran to the edge of the ring and suckerpunched Bell in the stomach. Caught off-guard, the monstrous man doubled over as the wind had been knocked out of him. Clark ran around the outside of the ring to stop Koloff but was met by a wooden chair to his skull. As if that weren't enough damage, Koloff pushed Clark against the nearest wall and proceeded to punch him repeatedly. To Koloff's surprise, Wentworth, the man he was trying to help, pulled him away from Clark.

"Get out of here!" Wentworth yelled. "Come back tomorrow! Come back tomorrow!"

Why is he angry with me? a confused Koloff thought. *I'm*

trying to help him.

The next day, still disoriented from the previous night's events, Koloff came back to the gym for his first training session. Wentworth instructed him to get dressed for action and wait in the ring. Koloff did as he was told and waited patiently for Wentworth to emerge. Only one problem—it wasn't Wentworth who emerged but the same Sailor Clark that Koloff had attacked the night before. "He had this big knot on his head, and he looked angry," Koloff says. "If looks could kill, I'd be dead. He got in the ring and

"He had this big knot on his head, and he looked angry. If looks could kill, I'd be dead. . . . I was scared. I was convinced that I was going to get beat up and I was going to have to take it because I wanted to be a wrestler."

kicked the ropes, pounded the mat, pulled on the ropes, and then he looked at me. I was scared. I was convinced that I was going to get beat up and I was going to have to take it because I wanted to be a wrestler."

Clark sensed Koloff's fear and started to back off. He let the young wrestler-to-be off the hook but not without a stern warning and subsequent education on the rules of professional wrestling. "You can't get involved in matches when you're a fan," Clark told him. "It's none of your business."

Koloff was also "smartened up" on the theatrical side of wrestling. Up to that point, he believed it was completely real, as did most fans. It would not be until Koloff was close to retirement that the industry would break the code of silence that protected wrestling's secrets. For the next six months, Koloff trained in Hamilton with the hopes of becoming like his wrestling idol, Bruno Sammartino. He quickly earned the nicknames "stiffy" and "crowbar" due to his solid, stiff, in-ring style. Koloff's passion for wrestling often caused him to hit, kick, and grab his opponents harder than necessary.

Koloff had just turned nineteen when Wentworth decided he was ready for action. He traveled to the northeastern U.S. for five shots with Vince McMahon Sr. and the World Wide Wrestling Federation. Koloff's first match was televised, a rarity in the wrestling business at that time. A bigger shock came when that night's card was released.

"I was told just before the match that I was in the fourth spot, and I was going to be up against Bruno Sammartino," Koloff says. "I almost had a heart attack. He was my hero, and I was very nervous. Some of the old guys called me to the side. I don't know if they were trying to instigate something or if they were really trying to advise me, but they all made sure to tell me what to do."

"Hey, kid," one veteran warned the newcomer. "You're not going to have much time out there. You'd better get some licks in. Attack him if you get a chance."

Koloff was educated in Sammartino's pre-match routine, which included the legend dropping to one knee and making the sign of the cross. Koloff took the advice and literally ran Sammartino over before he could get back on his feet. He had his opponent in the

ropes and started kicking him harder than normal. Koloff didn't want him to get back up. But predictably, Sammartino managed to regain his composure and promptly ended the match in mere seconds.

"I was told just before the match that I was in the fourth spot, and I was going to be up against Bruno Sammartino. I almost had a heart attack. He was my hero . . ."

"He picked me up and slammed me to the mat with a backdrop," Koloff remembers. "I don't think I'd ever taken that move before. Then he put me in the bear hug. As soon as he squeezed me, I didn't have to be told to give up. He was very strong."

After wrestling in major cities such as Pittsburgh, Washington, and New York, Koloff headed back to Canada, where he continued to improve his skills. By the mid 1960s, he had made another move, this time to the West Coast, where he wrestled in Vancouver, Portland, and Seattle. Koloff also made his first trip to Japan. In 1967, he went to Montreal, where he became the Canadian national champion. Koloff credits promoter Jacque Rougeau for creating his infamous Russian character. Rougeau had researched the history books and discovered a Dan Koloff who had wrestled in Montreal thirty years earlier. Rougeau also noticed an eerie resemblance between Koloff and Russian socialist Vladimir Lenin. The one catch? Koloff would have to shave his head bald to complete the gimmick. After having a few too many drinks with his brothers one night and recklessly mentioning the idea to them, the deed was done.

"I woke up the next morning, and I had a roll of toilet paper all over my head," Koloff says with a chuckle. "They'd shaved my head and done a pretty crude job."

His success in Montreal once again opened the door to New York and the WWWF. His first manager was Tony Angelo, who moved to New York with Koloff but became seriously ill and returned to Montreal. His contract was sold to Captain Lou Albano, who would stay with Koloff throughout his WWWF days. After spending much of 1969 with the federation, he traveled to Australia and spent the better part of a year there. In January of 1971, Koloff was called back to New York. Sammartino was scheduled to wrestle a television title defense that night, but his opponent was unable to compete. By then, Sammartino's legend had

IVAN KOLOFF

grown to epic proportions. He had been the World Heavyweight Champion for seven and a half years without a single defeat. During Koloff's previous WWWF run, he had faced off with Sammartino numerous times. He had managed to defeat the Italian star by a technicality from time to time but never took the title. Now, with little warning or explanation, Koloff was given the task of taking Sammartino's belt. While he believes he was only being used as an "in-between" champion, it remains his defining moment as a professional wrestler.

"At that time, they were gearing Pedro Morales for that title shot," Koloff says. "But it made my career. Even though I didn't remain champion for long, it made me a name by wrestling in New York and holding the belt. When you wrestled Bruno, you became a name. To win the title from Bruno was a big deal. He was really over with the fans."

After a short three-week run, Koloff lost his title to Morales and never regained it. He would go on to spend time with Verne Gagne's American Wrestling Alliance (AWA) along with superstars such as Billy Robinson, Wahoo McDaniel, Dick Murdoch, Ric Flair, Ray Stevens, and Billy Graham. Koloff also spent time in the International Wrestling Alliance (IWA) and the Georgia Championship Wrestling, and briefly worked with Bill Watts in the Mid-South wrestling promotion. He also teamed with Mad Dog Vachon in Old Japan Wrestling to claim the Asian Tag Team title.

Koloff eventually landed with Jim Crockett's Mid-Atlantic

Championship Wrestling office in Charlotte, part of the old National Wrestling Alliance (NWA). It was the early 1980s, and he had yet to reclaim the glory days of his WWWF run.

Oddly enough, international politics helped change Koloff's fortunes. During the late 1970s and throughout much of the 1980s, anti-Soviet sentiments ran high in the U.S. Koloff's broken English, glazed with a Russian accent, was all it took to send fans into a heated frenzy. His red costume, complete with hammer and sickle insignia—not to mention Koloff's ability to verbally taunt the crowd—provided that extra grain of salt in the wound.

"The Cold War situation between Russia and the United States made it a natural," Koloff says. "There was always that tension. The people would root for anyone who wrestled against me, because I was the 'bad guy from Russia.' It didn't even have to be an American wrestler. It was the same when I was fighting a Canadian, a guy from England, or an Australian. They were still the good guy over me."

Koloff's next career boost came in the form of a young ex-college football star named Scott Simpson. While he had held NWA Tag Team titles with Ray Stevens and his current partner Don Kernodle (whose gimmick was that of a Soviet sympathizer), the introduction of a third team member would elevate Koloff to new heights. Simpson was introduced as Koloff's nephew Nikita Koloff, and the three began wreaking havoc throughout the federation. Eventually, Krusher Kruschev replaced Kernoble, and the new trio became NWA Six-Man World Tag Champions. Koloff trained his new partner on the fly, often working out routines and moves in the car traveling to events and in the locker room just before matches. All of the hard work put into his protégé was short-lived, however, as the NWA's biggest star, Dusty Rhodes, decided to take Nikita Koloff as his new partner.

"When [Nikita] came out with Dusty, that killed my income for a while," Koloff says. "For the two or three years before that, I worked with Nikita and helped get him over. I protected him in the ring also. If our team had to look bad, they looked bad through me. Dusty was in a position to make that decision, so I guess I can't blame him for that. But it did make a big dent in what I was doing."

"The Cold War situation between Russia and the United States made it a natural. There was always that tension. The people would root for anyone who wrestled against me, because I was the 'bad guy from Russia.'"

Koloff recovered with the formation of the Powers of Pain. He and new teammate Paul Jones battled the likes of the Road Warriors and the Assassins, but admittedly, it was the beginning of the end for Koloff and the NWA. The bookers tried to switch Koloff to a babyface, but it just didn't work. Trying to convince the fans to love one of wrestling's most hated heels was too much to ask. In 1989, Koloff decided to leave the promotion, which had become Ted Turner's World Championship Wrestling (WCW) six months earlier. The wrestlers and employees were asked to move to Atlanta, and Koloff had already settled into a comfortable life in North Carolina.

"It was just too much," Koloff says. "There was a slump in wrestling, and things hadn't taken off yet. As far as I was concerned, I wasn't fitting into the picture. It was time for me to move on and try the independent circuit."

Koloff spent the next five years traveling to Florida, the Philippines, Japan, Puerto Rico, and the West Indies. He capitalized on his popular Russian heel persona and was consistently booked almost every weekend. By the time Koloff was nearing retirement, an alcohol and drug abuse problem had been years in the making. It started as a subtle way of life back on the farm in Canada with social drinking at occasional family celebrations. Even as a teenager, he drank beer and wine into the late hours. As Koloff began his wrestling career, he looked at each night as a celebration of what he had accomplished in the ring. Celebrations always required the obligatory round of drinks.

"If I had a trip that took a hundred miles, I'd go out and buy a six-pack of beer," Koloff says. "If it was two hundred miles, I'd get a twelve-pack. I had a lot of long trips when I came home so drunk, I couldn't even remember driving. I became an alcoholic and didn't even know it. I wouldn't admit it."

In early 1970s Koloff was introduced to the drug culture. He had suffered a herniated disk while working in the AWA and took painkillers, muscle relaxers, and sleeping pills to avoid back surgery. When his prescription ran out, he found himself shopping street-corner "pharmacies" for relief. Koloff discovered hallucinogens as well, but that habit was short-lived. Instead, marijuana and strong liquor provided the next step in Koloff's tendency toward addiction.

"I was hooked, and I didn't even realize it," Koloff says. "I got progressively worse. I started getting more and more injuries. My knee was going out, and I broke both of my shoulders. I had bicep tears and tricep tears. Another disk went out in my back. My ankle broke three times. The drugs were causing a lot of that. I was in the ring half messed up, and I was doing stunts that it takes a great athlete to do without killing yourself."

"I was hooked, and I didn't even realize it. I got progressively worse. I started getting more and more injuries. . . . The drugs were causing a lot of that. I was in the ring half messed up, and I was doing stunts that it takes a great athlete to do without killing yourself."

Over the next two decades, Koloff survived countless incidents that could have resulted in his death. One night, on a two-hundred-mile road trip driving seventy miles per hour, he found himself in a ditch. He had passed out at the wheel. Minor car accidents were not uncommon, but a DWI charge that left his car wrapped around a telephone pole in 1989 was an eye-opener. Every time he survived such a close call, he always knew whom to thank.

"Thank You, Lord," Koloff recalls mumbling. "Lord Jesus, help me."

Those times always took him back to his childhood, when his

parents would make all ten children go to church every Sunday, without exception. Whether by horse and buggy in the summer or horse and sleigh in the win-ter, the Perras family traveled several miles to the nearest Catholic church. "Until I was a teenager, I was made to do that," Koloff says. "Then I rebelled against it. But it

"During the day, I found myself just talking to God and having a conversation with Him. 'Please take these burdens away,' I'd say. 'The alcohol. The drugs. The chewing tobacco.' Lo and behold, He took the desire from me and the need for that stuff."

always stuck with me. Later on, in my times of need, I called out to the Lord like many of us do, but I'd always go back to my old style of living. I never honored Christ. I just called out to Him when I needed help."

When Koloff retired in 1994, his problems outside of the ring didn't go away. His early wrestling career had already played a big part in a failed marriage. Now married to his second wife, Renee, he was concerned that the bad habits he picked up on the road might once again have a negative influence on his family.

"So many times I'd thrown the tobacco away and the marijuana," Koloff says. "I always went back and got more. Even the booze—I was so disgusted with myself. I think I was trying to kill myself but not brave enough to take the gun or knife and actually do it. I always thought that I was a tough guy. As a matter of fact, I know I was. I'd accomplished a lot for a little guy, but I couldn't stop doing this stuff. I was slowly killing myself."

It was 1996 when his old wrestling partner Nikita Koloff invited him to that revival service. Never known to be openly emotional, Nikita seemed different. "He was smiling and all excited," Koloff noticed. "It caught me off guard."

Nikita told him about an exciting evangelist named Terrance Rose, who was holding a revival at Faith Covenant Church. Koloff had slipped into the back, hoping he wouldn't be noticed. His concern quickly faded as he ran to the front and accepted Christ. Admittedly, it took some time for him to pursue the typical "Christian" things, but he noticed a change almost immediately.

"I'd find myself on the bed at night, and I'd start reading the Bible," Koloff says. "I was just drawn to it. During the day, I found myself just talking to God and having a conversation with Him. 'Please take these burdens away,' I'd say. 'The alcohol. The drugs. The chewing tobacco.' Lo and behold, He took the desire from me and the need for that stuff. It gave me some breathing room to deal with the other things that I had to do."

For Koloff, that means more involvement in the ministry. He no longer runs the wrestling school he opened after retiring, but he still appears at autograph sessions on a regular basis. Koloff donates much of his proceeds to charities and helps raise money for the Children's Miracle Network and the March of Dimes. But that's just the beginning. Koloff is looking to get more involved with local Bible studies and hopes to spend more time sharing his testimony in churches, detention halls, prisons, and beyond. It may have taken him nearly fifty years to get to this point, but Koloff realizes that it's better late than never when it comes to personal and spiritual fulfillment.

"The only way I'll be happy is if I'm serving the Lord," he says.

IVAN KOLOFF

iVAN KOLOFF

FULL NAME: Ivan Koloff (legally changed from Jim Perras)

NICKNAMES: The Russian Bear

BIRTHDATE: August 25, 1942

BIRTHPLACE: Nation River Valley, Ontario

HOMETOWN: Winterville, North Carolina

HEIGHT: 5'10"

WEIGHT: 225 lbs.

FAMILY: Renee (wife); four children; seven grandchildren

PRO WRESTLING DEBUT: Fall of 1961 in Pittsburgh, Pennsylvania

FIRST MATCH: Lost to Bruno Sammartino

PROMOTIONS: AWA, WWWF, NWA, WCW, JWA, Old Japan, Georgia Championship, FCW, WWC

TITLES HELD: WWWF World Heavyweight, NWA World Tag Team (w/ Ray Stevens, w/ Don Kernodle, w/ Nikita Koloff 2x, Manny Fernandez), NWA Six-Man Tag Team (w/ Nikita Koloff and Krusher Krushchev; w/ The Powers of Pain), WWC Heavyweight, Canadian Heavyweight, Canadian International Heavyweight (2x); Asian Tag Team (w/ Mad Dog Vachon), Florida Tag Team (w/ Pat Patterson, w/ Nikolai Volkoff, w/ Mr. Saito 3x), Georgia Tag Team (w/ Alexis Smirnoff, w/ Ole Anderson 5x); Mid-Atlantic Heavyweight; Southern Heavyweight; Mid-Atlantic Television (3x); Mid-Atlantic Heavyweight; JWA World Tag Team (w/ Mad Dog Vachon); WWA World Heavyweight

GEORGE SOUTH

CHAPTER 10

GEORGE SOUTH

CHAPTER 10

 eorge South was expecting something a bit more glamorous than the old, decrepit warehouse he was approaching. It was more like a scene from a campy "B" movie. Undaunted, he opened the door and was welcomed by an obnoxiously loud creaking sound. As he cautiously peered into the building, South noticed a motley crew already working out in the ring. An old man, a large Samoan, and a midget diverted their attention to the wide-eyed eighteen-year old kid who had just entered their world.

"You wanna be a rassler?" the old man inquired.

Before the man could form a satisfactory reply, South jumped into the ring still wearing his blue jeans and work boots.

"This is gonna be pretty easy," South thought to himself.

But before the smirk on South's face could develop into a full-blown smile, the old man grabbed the youngster and began applying a variety of wrestling holds. He stretched his body in ways he never knew it could be stretched and put him in every kind of knot imaginable. Next, it was the Samoan's turn. For the next hour, South took a series of harsh bumps from the dark-skinned giant. South only *thought* he knew how to fall. Hours of watching televised wrestling matches hadn't paid off.

With torn jeans and a bloodied mouth, South collapsed in a corner of the ring. The unsympathetic trio added insult to injury with a collective hearty laugh. The most diminutive of the three walked over to where South lay. Expecting a helping hand from the little guy, South was instead greeted by a kick to the ribs that hurt harder than anything he'd felt that day. He fell out of the ring onto his head, then gingerly crawled to the door.

"From the first day I went to that training building answering an ad in the paper, I knew I was gonna be a rassler," South says with a thick North Carolina accent. "But after they beat me up, I didn't ever want to come back. But the next day, I walked right back in that place. Why I went back, I don't know."

Rusty Roberts was the "old man" who first trained South. One week later, South participated in his first match for Roberts' now-defunct Eastern Championship Wrestling. His aging and out-of-shape opponent, not so aptly named "The Blonde Sweetheart," lost the match after succumbing to heat exhaustion and vomiting all over South. Regurgitated dinner and all, South's dream had come true. He was a bona fide professional "rassler." Two decades later, South better understands why he didn't give up after that first grueling day. It turns out that South has found his destiny within the squared circle, a ministry he never imagined would come to pass.

By most standards, South had a rough childhood, though he doesn't see it that way. Born the youngest of thirteen in Boone, North Carolina, South was raised in the hills. His parents were both killed in a car accident when he was six, and he spent the next several months bouncing around between brothers and sisters and other relatives. He finally ended up in Gastonia, North Carolina, with older brother Bob. South was rebellious as a youngster, which landed him in all kinds of trouble until two major changes took place in his young life: He discovered professional wrestling, and he discovered God. His brother led him to Christ; the wrestling came by way of the television.

"I knew I was gonna be a rassler. But after they beat me up, I didn't ever want to come back. But the next day, I walked right back in that place. Why I went back, I don't know."

South's idol was Paul Jones, one of Mid-Atlantic Championship Wrestling's biggest stars. The two have since become close friends. But during the 1970s, when kids could still wait outside the arenas for their heroes to arrive and walk inside with them, South became well known among the wrestlers. He would routinely pace the parking lot or just inside the arena, hoping to catch some time with Jones.

"The old-timers got so used to seeing me around, and they'd play a joke on me and tell me that Paul wasn't going to be there," South recalls. "I just knew that I'd heard it on the news. I'd get to crying, and they'd all be laughing at me. They'd make me fightin' mad! Finally, Paul would walk in, and the old guys would just laugh."

Despite his brother's encouragement, South grew up with the concept that church consisted of "old people who wanted money." He had accepted Christ at a young age but never acted on it. Instead, South filled the void in his life with high school athletics. There, he saw three years of action as an amateur wrestler. Much to South's dismay, it wasn't the same kind of wrestling he was expecting. "Where's the ropes at?" a naïve South asked his coach on the first day of practice.

His misconception of the sport was matched only by his misconception of church. South's negative images stayed with him for several years. He had just started his wrestling career when he married a woman named Missy. South had only been to church twice since moving to Gastonia, once for a service and once for his wedding. A medical problem that affected their newborn son, George Jr., would end that streak. George Jr. was scheduled for eye surgery the next morning, and Missy suggested they go to a church service for support. Reedy Creek Baptist Church in Charlotte was then nothing more than a handful of people who met in an American Legion building. South reluctantly went along with his wife and baby.

"I'll go," South retorted. "But I'm sittin' on the back row. I ain't shakin' no hands. When they finish, I'm leaving!"

True to his word, South endured the service, then immediately bolted through the front door at its conclusion. The next morning, he and Missy drove to downtown

"I'll go," South retorted. *"But I'm sittin' on the back row. I ain't shakin' no hands. When they finish, I'm leaving!"*

Charlotte with their baby. To South's surprise, Pastor David Wilson from Reedy Creek Baptist was already at the hospital, anticipating their arrival. The preacher was greeted by South's less-than-friendly attitude. "I hadn't given any money the night before," South says. *He's come to collect the money!* he thought at the time.

Wilson offered to pray for George Jr. before the surgery. The disgruntled father agreed, then immediately sent the pastor on his way. After the baby's successful eye surgery, the family returned home. But all was not well with South. The rest of the week, he had many sleepless nights. No one had ever gone out of their way for South. He was shaken by Wilson's act of kindness. After calling the pastor and asking him why he came to the hospital, South became curious about the church. He wanted to see what was going on down there. He and Missy visited from time to time, then eventually made the plunge and became members. South has since rededicated his life to Christ and has been teaching a Sunday school class for more than three years.

South's spiritual growth came along much faster than his wrestling career. He spent the next six years finding work wherever he could: high school gyms, street corners, backyards, anywhere he could find someone who would let him get in the ring. South occasionally paid promoters just for a shot to wrestle in front of the smallest of audiences. It was that same concept that first landed South on television. While working for Mid-Atlantic, he was asked if he would like to be on the Turner Broadcasting System (TBS) program. South eagerly jumped at the chance, paying a booking fee to get in front of the camera. Many veteran wrestlers frowned upon the practice, but South knew it was his best and perhaps only chance. That night he faced Ric Flair and was so nervous that he fell from the top rope during a routine move. Everyone laughed, but South couldn't have cared less. He was "rasslin'" on TV.

After finding steady work with Mid-Atlantic Wrestling, South's career began to expand as promoter Jim Crockett's business grew.

GEORGE SOUTH

Things really took off for South when Crockett and Dusty Rhodes took over Georgia Championship Wrestling. He started to work six and even seven days a week. South also benefited from not having an exclusive contract with any of the federations. On any given weekend, he could be seen on television wrestling for WCW, WWF, and Bill Watts' Universal Wrestling Federation (UWF). But South's most prized moments came in matches that involved his hero, Paul Jones. Already retired from ring action, Jones was acting as a manager when South broke in with Mid-Atlantic. South still treasures those matches against Jones' protégés.

"I used to tell guys to throw me out of the ring so I could go to Paul Jones and let him hit me," South says. "I'd seen him throw that punch for years. Sometimes I'd stay out on the floor going to him more than I was in the ring. At the time, I was still in awe of him."

> On any given weekend, [South] could be seen on television wrestling for WCW, WWF, and Bill Watts' Universal Wrestling Federation (UWF).

South was having the time of his life. He was getting beaten by some of the best in the business. He especially remembers the multiple beatings he took at the hands of former WWF superstar The Ultimate Warrior. South was left unconscious several times due to his opponent's vicious clothesline. One of those hits was immortalized on the box of a WWF toy wrestling ring. "Every time I want to be reminded of how hard he hit me, I go look at that box," South jokes.

Not one for the party scene, South avoided many of the pitfalls associated with the sports and entertainment fields. He never found the drug scene appealing and admits he was too "goofy" to realize if any women were trying to create marital strife. But South is not without regrets.

"My biggest regret is that I've wasted a lot of time," South says. "I've been all over the world, and I've traveled with the likes of Hogan and Flair. I should have been telling guys about the Lord instead of trying to get what I could out of rasslin'. I've always tried to please God first, but I haven't always done it. I'm trying not to make the same mistakes again."

One instance that South does not regret is the time he shared his faith with Hulk Hogan while still in the WWF. The world-famous wrestler was then known for telling his younger fans to say their prayers and take their vitamins. South wanted to know if Hogan was for real but struggled to muster the courage to approach him. For two days, South trailed Hogan, waiting for the right opportunity. Finally, on his last day of work with the federation, he followed Hogan downstairs to the commissary. "Lord, just give me the strength to ask him," South prayed silently before approaching the Hulkster.

"Hulk, I'd like to share this tract with you," South said, handing him a gospel pamphlet.

"Man, I needed this," Hogan, a professing Christian, replied. "You know, I get on TV and tell kids to say their prayers, but when I pray, I'm the same size as those kids are."

While working for WCW during the mid 1990s, South made a decision to start incorporating his faith into wrestling. He had "John 3:16" sewn onto the back of his wrestling tights so everyone would know he was a Christian. The move was not well received by the federation's bookers or executives. Feeling like he'd "smacked somebody's mamma," South was asked to turn his trunks inside out for the television taping. He reluctantly complied but vowed to never do television again if he couldn't display his faith.

"My biggest regret is that I've wasted a lot of time. I've been all over the world, and I've traveled with the likes of Hogan and Flair. I should have been telling guys about the Lord instead of trying to get what I could out of rasslin'."

Once again, South was watching the wrestling industry change before his eyes; vagabond wrestlers like him were finding fewer options with the two major federations, WWF and WCW. He and Gary Sabaugh (a.k.a. The Italian Stallion) started their own organization, simply known as the Professional Wrestling Federation (PWF). South and Sabaugh headlined most shows as bitter foes, then eventually as a championship tag team.

By 1999, the operation had shut down, making way for South's newest venture, the Exodus Wrestling Alliance (EWA). This time, ministry would be the primary focus. South continues to use the EWA as a way to share his testimony and hundreds of Bibles with young and old alike.

"People ask, 'How in the world can you be a Christian and be a professional rassler?'" South says. "When you talk to Christians about rasslin', the only thing they think of is the WWF. They can't even comprehend that there's seventy years of rasslin' history way before Vince McMahon started doing this junk that he's doing. There's actually a good side to rasslin'. Most people just think it's the women and the cussing. Basically, that doesn't have anything to do with rasslin'."

South owns three wrestling rings and uses them often for his ministry. Parents drop their kids off before the show so they can spend time watching South set up his ring and prepare for that night's matches. He shares more of the Bible and less of the wrestling talk that they come expecting. South also distributes a series of comic-book-style tracts illustrated by former DC Comics artist Nate Butler. Each of the three tracts uses wrestling analogies to convey a gospel message, with South (looking more like a superhero than an independent wrestler) as the messenger.

Every weekend, the EWA sets up shop in gymnasiums and

armories throughout North Carolina and surrounding areas. South has seen busloads of youth pull into the parking lots; most of the juveniles have a tendency to "throw up their middle fingers" throughout the festivities. He's been asked where Austin 3:16 is in the Bible and tries not to laugh at the confused reference to WWF wrestler "Stone Cold" Steve Austin's mockery of the popular scripture. Some see the inscription on his trunks and think his name is John and that he was born on March 16. Every night after the final match, South quickly grabs the microphone and jumps into his personal testimony. He hopes his words will capture someone's heart, just as much as he hopes the wrestling action captured their imaginations.

"People ask, 'How in the world can you be a Christian and be a professional rassler?' . . . They can't even comprehend that there's seventy years of rasslin' history way before Vince McMahon started doing this junk that he's doing. . . . Basically, that doesn't have anything to do with rasslin'."

South often tells his onlookers about the power of prayer. It's a concept that he practices in every aspect of his life. Take, for instance, South's trip to Texas in the year 2000. A die-hard Dallas Cowboys fan, South prayed for two months that God would allow him to see Texas Stadium. He was traveling to Brownwood for a youth rally with Ted DiBiase, and on the way they drove by the stadium, fulfilling South's dream. After leading several young people to make commitments to Christ in Brownwood, South and his friends left early to take one last look at the historic venue. They drove around the boarded-up stadium for a while, until an older gentleman in a golf cart approached their car and asked them if they needed help.

What happened next still gives South a severe case of goose-bumps. He revealed his secret desire to tour Texas Stadium. Much to South's surprise, the groundskeeper led the men to the gate and opened it up, letting them in for an exclusive tour. They walked on the field, checked out the locker rooms, and even spent time in team owner Jerry

"I used to tell God, 'You'd give me one big year, I'll do so much work for You, and I'll build churches.' The Lord knew I was lying through my teeth. . . . I'm so glad that God has had His hand on m for my whole career."

Jones' private skybox. As South left one of his tracts on a stadium seat, he wondered if anyone would believe his story. For proof, South asked the groundskeeper for a souvenir, namely one of the actual seats out of Texas Stadium. His request was perfectly timed. The old man retrieved one of the seats that had recently been replaced and handed it to South. "I've been a groundskeeper for fifty years," he told South. "I can't remember the last time I've been at the stadium at six o'clock in the morning." South, though, knew exactly why he had picked that day to show up for work early.

"The little blessings that God has given me through rasslin', I can't put a price tag on that," South says. "Even if God hadn't allowed me to go inside that stadium, it wouldn't make Him any less God. I just honestly believe, you can't pray about cancer or your kids or anything else if you can't pray about something little that just means something to you and God."

South hopes he never has to give up wrestling. His training school in Concord is yet another way he tries to pass on his knowledge of the business and, more importantly, his love for Jesus. South knows he will never be as famous as The Rock or Stone Cold. However, he does take comfort in knowing that the lasting impact he makes on those around him has been directed by a greater force than anything fame or fortune could ever afford.

"I used to tell God, 'If You'd give me one big year, I'll do so much work for You, and I'll build churches,'" South says. "The Lord knew I was lying through my teeth. He knew that if He gave me one good year, I'd forget Him. I'm so glad that God has had His hand on me for my whole career."

GEORGE SOUTH

FULL NAME: George Edward South

NICKNAMES: Iron Man Mark Thunder; Gorgeous; Mr. Number One

BIRTHDATE: September 7, 1962

BIRTHPLACE: Boone, North Carolina

HOMETOWN: Concord, North Carolina

HEIGHT: 6'0"

WEIGHT: 242 lbs.

FAMILY: Missy (wife), George Jr., Brock, and Garrett (sons), Abigail & Scarlet (twin daughters)

PRO WRESTLING DEBUT: December 16, 1981

FIRST MATCH: Defeated the Blonde Sweetheart (Gastonia, North Carolina, for Eastern Championship Wrestling)

PROMOTIONS: WCW, NWA, WWF, Mid-Atlantic Championship, Georgia Championship, UWF, Tri-States, SMW, PWF (Pro Wrestling Federation), ECW (Eastern Championship Wrestling), EWA

TITLES HELD: NWA West Coast Tag Team (w/Gary Royal); PWF Heavyweight, PWF Tag Team (w/The Italian Stallion); PWF Junior Heavyweight; SMW Television; EWA World Heavyweight

FINISHING MOVE: Swinging neck breaker

BEST FEUD: vs. the Italian Stallion

WORST INJURY: Cracked ribs; knocked unconscious multiple times

Appendix A

PROFESSIONAL WRESTLING TERMS

Angle: Written plot or storyline.

Babyface: Wrestler portraying a good guy; also called a "face."

Backdrop: Wrestling move in which one wrestler richochets his opponent off the ropes, plants his hands into his opponent's back, then flips his opponent over his head and onto his back.

Blading: Act of self-inflicting wounds during the course of a wrestling match in order to draw blood.

Booker: Person responsible for deciding the outcome of matches; also called a "writer."

Boston Crab: Submission hold in which wrestler tucks his opponent's legs under his armpits then turns the wrestler over onto his stomach without letting go. The wrestler then applies pressure by assuming a sit-down position.

Broadway: Match that ends in a draw or has no winner.

Bump: Slang for when a wrestler takes a fall.

Camel Clutch: Wrestling move in which one wrestler has his opponent face down on the mat then stands over him, places the opponent's arms on his thighs and grips his chin with both hands. The wrestler then pulls back, applying pressure to the chin and neck.

Clothesline: Wrestling move in which wrestler's forearm connects with opponent's upper body (i.e. head, neck, chest, etc.).

Fallaway Slam: Wrestling move in which wrestler lifts opponent across the back on his stomach then falls backwards while holding onto him.

Federation: Wrestling organization.

Feud: Extended dispute between two wrestlers or two groups of wrestlers.

Figure Four Leglock: Wrestling hold in which wrestler locks legs with opponent (while both lie on the mat) and then applies pressure by leaning back.

Finishing Move: High impact maneuver that results in a victory.

Gimmick: Wrestling persona or character.

Heel: Wrestler who portrays the bad guy or acts in a manner that will cause wrestling fans to dislike him.

Hip Toss: Wrestling move in which wrestler locks arms with his opponent (who is to his side) then flips him to the mat on his back.

House Show: Non-televised wrestling event.

Jobber: Wrestler who consistently loses matches to more popular wrestlers.

Kayfabe: Code of silence in which wrestlers do not share wrestling secrets or future outcomes of matches and story-lines.

Leg Drop: Wrestling move in which wrestler literally drops his leg in a downward motion onto his opponent's upper body (chest or throat region).

Lucha Libre: Mexican term for "professional wrestling."

Mid-carder: Wrestler who is a step below the top level or "main event" status.

Moonsault: Wrestling move in which wrestler stands on the top rope, performs a back flip, then lands on the opponent

Over: Describes when a wrestler's character is loved (if a baby-face) or hated (if a heel).

Pop: Positive crowd response.

Promotion: Wrestling organization.

Run-in: When a wrestler/group of wrestlers abruptly interrupts and interferes with another match.

Shoot: Non-staged wrestling event; truth-based interview or angle.

Sleeper Hold: Submission hold in which wrestler locks his one forearm around opponent's forehead and the other forearm around his throat in order to cut off the blood and oxygen flow to the brain and render him unconscious.

Stable: Group of wrestlers who consistently work as a team (i.e. The Four Horsemen).

Storyline: Written plot or story that takes place within a wrestling setting.

Squared Circle: Slang term for "wrestling ring."

Submission Hold: Wrestling move in which opponent cannot escape and must give up.

Swerve: Unexpected happening or twist to the predicted outcome of a match or angle/storyline.

Swinging Neckbreaker: Wrestling move in which wrestler faces opponent, bends him over and places his head under the left armpit then with the right hand, grabs the opponent's free arm and swings the opponent over onto his back. Both wrestlers land on their back following this move.

Territory: Precursor to promotions/federations (i.e. Kansas City territory, Amarillo territory, etc.).

Turn: When a wrestler makes a sudden change from babyface to heel or vice versa.

Turnbuckle: Padding on the corner of a wrestling ring that overlays the ropes.

Valet: Female escort for a wrestler.

Vignette: Short pre-recorded promotional video.

Work: Staged or pre-planned wrestling event or interview.

Appendix B
PROFESSIONAL WRESTLING ORGANIZATIONS

AAA . . . . Asistencia Asesoria Administracion

ACCW . . . . Atlantic Coast Championship Wrestling

AJPW . . . . All Japan Professional Wrestling

AWA . . . . American Wrestling Association

CCW . . . . Carolina Championship Wrestling

CMLL . . . . Consejo Mundial de Lucha Libre

CPW . . . . California Professional Wrestling

CPW . . . . Championship Professional Wrestling

CWA . . . . Continental Wrestling Association

CWF . . . . Championship Wrestling of Florida

ECW . . . . Eastern Championship Wrestling

ECW . . . . Extreme Championship Wrestling

EMLL . . . . Empresa Mundial de Lucha Libre

EWA . . . . Exodus Wrestling Alliance

FCW . . . . Florida Championship Wrestling

FOW . . . . Future of Wrestling

FWA . . . . Florida Wrestling Alliance

HWO . . . . Hollywood Wrestling Office

IPWA . . . . Independent Pro Wrestling Alliance

IWA . . . . Independent Wrestling Alliance

IWF	International Wrestling Federation
IWF	Independent Wrestling Federation
MCW	Memphis Championship Wrestling
NJWA	New Japan Professional Wrestling
NWA	National Wrestling Alliance
NWO	New World Order
PWA	Power Wrestling Association
PWF	Pro Wrestling of Florida
PWF	Professional Wrestling Federation
SAPW	South Atlantic Pro Wrestling
SCW	Southern Championship Wrestling
SMW	Smoky Mountain Wrestling
UCW	Unified Championship Wrestling
USWA	United States Wrestling Association
UWF	Universal Wrestling Federation
WCW	World Championship Wrestling
WSA	Western States Alliance
WWA	World Wrestling Alliance
WWC	World Wrestling Council
WWF	World Wrestling Federation
WWW	World Wide Wrestling
WWWF	World Wide Wrestling Federation
XPW	Xtreme Professional Wrestling

Appendix C
FEATURED WRESTLERS' CONTACT INFORMATION

B Brian Blair

brianblair@brianblair.com
www.brianblair.com

Tully Blanchard

c/o The Exodus Foundation
2971 NC 108 Hwy.
Rutherfordton, NC 28139
(828) 288-1011

Ted DiBiase

c/o Heart of David Ministries
P.O. Box 1291
Clinton, MS 39060
www.milliondollarman.com

Hector Guerrero

guerrerohector@juno.com

Ivan Koloff

P.O. Box 2673
Winterville, NC 28590
www.ivankoloff.com

Nikita Koloff
c/o Koloff for Christ Ministries
P.O. Box 424
Mount Pleasant, NC 28124
nikita@nikitakoloff.com
www.nikitakoloff.com

Bruno Sassi
c/o Hollywood First Assembly of God
1019 N. 24th Ave.
Hollywood, FL 33020
(954) 922-5546
PHIDELTASLAM@hotmail.com

George South
c/o Exodus Wrestling Alliance
3638 Farm Lake Drive
Concord, NC 28027

Sting
c/o Santa Clarita Church on the Rock
(661) 251-7625

Tatanka
(727) 866-9716 (FAX)
cnment@earthlink.net
www.nativetatanka.com

ABOUT THE AUTHOR

Chad Bonham is an eleven-year journalism veteran, who began writing at age nineteen while attending the University of Tulsa. Chad has written for *CCM*, *7 Ball*, *Release*, *Profile*, *New Man*, *Christian Retailing*, *Ministries Today*, and several other national publications. A longtime wrestling fan, Chad wrote his first cover story on Steve Borden—better known as Sting. That issue of *New Man* was one of the magazine's best-selling newsstand issues ever and inspired Chad to write *Wrestling with God*.

Chad is the program director and on-air personality for Live 101.5 (KMRX FM), a Christian CHR/Rock radio station. He has been actively involved in music for twenty-two years as a singer, songwriter, and professional drummer. Chad is currently a member of David Welch & Sixsteps and also plays with the worship band in his home church.

Chad holds a Bachelor of Arts in Communications and currently lives with his wife, Amy, in Broken Arrow, Oklahoma. Chad can be contacted by e-mail at *WrestlingWithGod@aol.com*.

Additional copies of this book and other titles by RiverOak
Publishing are available from your local bookstore.

If you have enjoyed this book, or if it has impacted your life,
we would like to hear from you.

Please contact us at:
RiverOak Publishing
Department E
P.O. Box 700143
Tulsa, Oklahoma 74170-0143

Or by e-mail at:
info@riveroakpublishing.com

Visit our website at:
www.riveroakpublishing.com